THE RECOVERY OF WONDER

McGILL-QUEEN'S STUDIES IN THE HISTORY OF IDEAS
Series Editor: Philip J. Cercone

1 Problems of Cartesianism
Edited by Thomas M. Lennon, John M. Nicholas, and John W. Davis

2 The Development of the Idea of History in Antiquity
Gerald A. Press

3 Claude Buffier and Thomas Reid
Two Common-Sense Philosophers
Louise Marcil-Lacoste

4 Schiller, Hegel, and Marx
State, Society, and the Aesthetic Ideal of Ancient Greece
Philip J. Kain

5 John Case and Aristotelianism in Renaissance England
Charles B. Schmitt

6 Beyond Liberty and Property
The Process of Self-Recognition in Eighteenth-Century Political Thought
J.A.W. Gunn

7 John Toland: His Methods, Manners, and Mind
Stephen H. Daniel

8 Coleridge and the Inspired Word
Anthony John Harding

9 The Jena System, 1804–5
Logic and Metaphysics
G.W.F. Hegel
Translation edited by John W. Burbidge and George di Giovanni
Introduction and notes by H.S. Harris

10 Consent, Coercion, and Limit
The Medieval Origins of Parliamentary Democracy
Arthur P. Monahan

11 Scottish Common Sense in Germany, 1768–1800
A Contribution to the History of Critical Philosophy
Manfred Kuehn

12 Paine and Cobbett
The Transatlantic Connection
David A. Wilson

13 Descartes and the Enlightenment
Peter A. Schouls

14 Greek Scepticism
Anti-Realist Trends in Ancient Thought
Leo Groarke

15 The Irony of Theology and the Nature of Religious Thought
Donald Wiebe

16 Form and Transformation
A Study in the Philosophy of Plotinus
Frederic M. Schroeder

17 From Personal Duties towards Personal Rights
Late Medieval and Early Modern Political Thought, c.1300–1600
Arthur P. Monahan

18 The Main Philosophical Writings and the Novel *Allwill*
Friedrich Heinrich Jacobi
Translated and edited by George di Giovanni

19 Kierkegaard as Humanist
Discovering My Self
Arnold B. Come

20 Durkheim, Morals, and Modernity
W. Watts Miller

21 The Career of Toleration
John Locke, Jonas Proast, and After
Richard Vernon

22 Dialectic of Love
Platonism in Schiller's Aesthetics
David Pugh

23 History and Memory in Ancient Greece
Gordon Shrimpton

24 Kierkegaard as Theologian
Recovering My Self
Arnold B. Come

25 An Enlightenment Tory in Victorian Scotland
The Career of Sir Archibald Alison
Michael Michie

26 The Road to Egdon Heath
The Aesthetics of the Great in Nature
Richard Bevis

27 Jena Romanticism and Its Appropriation of Jakob Böhme
Theosophy – Hagiography – Literature
Paolo Mayer

28 Enlightenment and Community
Lessing, Abbt, Herder, and the Quest for a German Public
Benjamin W. Redekop

29 Jacob Burckhardt and the Crisis of Modernity
John R. Hinde

30 The Distant Relation
Time and Identity in Spanish-American Fiction
Eoin S. Thomson

31 Mr Simson's Knotty Case
Divinity, Politics, and Due Process in Early Eighteenth-Century Scotland
Anne Skoczylas

32 Orthodoxy and Enlightenment
George Campbell in the Eighteenth Century
Jeffrey M. Suderman

33 Contemplation and Incarnation
The Theology of Marie-Dominique Chenu
Christophe F. Potworowski

34 Democratic Legitimacy
Plural Values and Political Power
Frederick M. Barnard

35 Herder on Nationality, Humanity, and History
Frederick M. Barnard

36 Labeling People
French Scholars on Society, Race, and Empire, 1815–1848
Martin S. Staum

37 The Subaltern Appeal to Experience
Self-Identity, Late Modernity, and the Politics of Immediacy
Craig Ireland

38 The Invention of Journalism Ethics
The Path to Objectivity and Beyond
Stephen J.A. Ward

39 The Recovery of Wonder
The New Freedom and the Asceticism of Power
Kenneth L. Schmitz

THE RECOVERY OF WONDER

The New Freedom and the Asceticism of Power

Kenneth L. Schmitz

McGill-Queen's University Press
Montreal & Kingston · London · Ithaca

ISBN 0-7735-2857-1 (cloth)
ISBN 0-7735-2858-x (paper)

Legal deposit second quarter 2005
Bibliothèque nationale du Québec

Printed in Canada on acid-free paper that is 100% ancient forest free (100% post-consumer recycled), processed chlorine free.

This book has been published with the help of a grant from the Canadian Federation for the Humanities and Social Sciences, through the Aid to Scholarly Publications Programme, using funds provided by the Social Sciences and Humanities Research Council of Canada.

McGill-Queen's University Press acknowledges the support of the Canada Council for the Arts for our publishing program. We also acknowledge the financial support of the Government of Canada through the Book Publishing Industry Development Program (BPIDP) for our publishing activities.

Library and Archives Canada Cataloguing in Publication

Schmitz, Kenneth L.
The recovery of wonder: the new freedom and the ascetism of power / Kenneth L. Schmitz.

(McGill-Queen's studies in the history of ideas; 39)
Includes index.
ISBN 0-7735-2857-1 (bound)
ISBN 0-7735-2858-x (pbk.)

1. Philosophy. I. Title. II. Series.

BD21.S35 2005 190 C2004-906135-6

This book was typeset by Interscript Inc.
in 10/12 Baskerville.

Dedicated with admiration and affection
to my friend and colleague of many years,
Jude Patrick Dougherty

Contents

Prologue

THE NARRATIVE that follows is not simply a recapitulation of a particular development in the history of Western thought and culture; it is primarily a *diagnostic*. For it seeks to point out what needs to be rethought at the fundamental levels of our present situation. The critical aspect is not meant to be a complaint, however; my purpose is rather to offer an ontologic of culture that may help to open up new avenues of thought and appreciation. No doubt, we must learn from other cultures; indeed, the ambiguity of the present globalization is not wholly without positive opportunities for a broader and deeper understanding, not only of humanity and its variety, but of our own precarious situation. We will not learn anything important, however, if we abandon our own history and surrender ourselves to the logic operative in the present process. We must not, in a fit of self-abasement, disregard the great gains in knowledge and liberty, those very developments that have come under the blight of postmodernist criticism. But postmodernism is correct in this: that we need to decentre the modern project. The trouble with most postmodern critique is that it begins with Descartes and reads what is pre- and post-Cartesian through the lens of the critical method; or, if not with Descartes, then with the Kant of the first *Critique*. In so doing, the postmodernists let the modern project define and pre-empt their counter-insurgency. And so their bite is not to the bone. Even Nietzsche is too reactive, letting modernity set the problematic and entering what is, for all its brilliance and biting humour, a myopic criticism.

The expansion of our glance beyond the modern horizon is already under way, not so much through postmodern criticism as through the efficacy of environmental concern. Indeed, it is in that concern that we hear the voice of nature itself, turning its own weapons upon us. Such an inconceivably immense force cannot be ignored or dominated for long. Fortunately, even our tentative efforts at respecting nature tend to show its forgiving generosity and its recuperative powers. Still, it will not tolerate abuse without exacting a price. We need, I will argue, to decentre the primacy of the modern project by replacing it with other modes of thought and appreciation. Specifically, we need to recover a strong enough sense of natural things in order to decentre, displace (but not abolish) the present project that understands nature, not as a community of things in which we participate, but as a field of mere objects, data, or phenomena for us to exploit.

The reflection upon the sense of *things* understood as *res*, that is, as realities in themselves, is intended not to be a mere repetition of past thought but rather a re-collection of a richer intellectual grasp of our present environs. The dark imponderability of the Greek cosmos and the rich inexhaustible mystery of the medieval universe can still throw light upon the fragility of our historical status and the problematic character of our demand for unrestricted precision control. They suggest that our legitimate demand for limited control of our environment must be applied with discrimination and respect for the things around us. It is a respect born of the recognition of our own freedom and power, and of the interior bond that we share with things.

Our culture is a rich one, and reflective archaeology of the past will bring forth treasures of yet some use for us. This calls for a new form of wisdom; on the cultural front, it means that we must in some measure become knowingly conscious of our own cultural trajectory in the midst of other cultures; and while we remain open to what we can learn from them, we must still cultivate an appreciation of our own. That care initiates an adventure in thought that may call for a new discipline, even an asceticism, in life and in the exercise of our new freedom. For thought alone is not enough. Wisdom is understanding that treats knowledge as something to be lived and not just thought. This perspective penetrates many dimensions of our life, including our adjustment to time. As part of a more fully human order, the new wisdom calls for a just balance of the moments of time, of what we owe to the past and to the future, as well as to the present. If we can as a culture succeed in such a task of thoughtful redress, we will have cultivated our new freedom well.

It is the question of how seriously we desire the fully human good. In Plato, ancient desire aspired to the good, with a recognition of the difficulty involved in the quest but also with a vision of the good as something attainable, even if as a gift from the gods. One of the great obstacles to reclaiming our own dignity through a just exercise of our new freedom is that modern and postmodern desire has built into it a frustration, a contradiction. For much of modern and especially postmodern desire harbours within it the will to a good which it thinks in its heart of hearts is unattainable. Though it is not likely to admit it, and in spite of itself, it evinces a bitter, self-denying nostalgia. My argument is that the ground of a new hope must pass through nature and nature's things; for that hope is grounded in a recognition of a certain transcendence in things that carries us beyond ourselves and our new-found power.

The proposal, then, is a call to thoughtful conversion through an approach to the world about us that responds to it as a gift and not simply as a given. The sensitivity to earlier passages of our history can provide us with a new appreciation of the fragility and the contingency of things, but this should only heighten the wonder of the actuality of those same things. The study of the "thingly" nature of things is meant to provide matter for a reflection upon the present state of affairs, and to see in things an interiority that is shared by both persons and things.

This is a traditional strategy, a strategy for recovering the wonder at the heart of things, not in a spirit of restoration or of revolution, but as a way of revisiting past sensibility insofar as it still lives with uncultivated possibilities for us. It is a sensibility the poets have never quite lost the feel of. This, surely, is the purpose of teaching the history of our culture, including those often inventive undergraduate courses in "Western Civ." It is the reason, too, for the study of the history of philosophy and, more generally, the history of thought. Is it not true that there remains something of significance and value in the past that still resonates in us? The aim, then, is to recover in a reflective mode of discourse that wonder out of which we might say anew with Shakespeare:

> In Nature's infinite book of secrecy
> A little I can read.

These reflections go back many years, indeed to my first publication in tribute to my mentor, Étienne Gilson, and they have since been fed by studies in modern and contemporary thought. It is, however, to the faculty, students, and friends of Trent University in Peterborough, Ontario, that I owe the first opportunity of presenting them in this more developed form. Their encouragement, through attendance and discussion at the Gilbert Ryle Lectures in 1997, has left its mark on the present revision and expansion. It is with especial thanks that I remember my one-time student, Professor Constantinos Boundas, and my long-time friend and colleague in Hegel studies, Professor John Burbidge, for their gracious hospitality. To these friends I happily add my appreciation of the efforts of John Zucchi and the readers and editorial staff at McGill-Queen's, who revived the project of publication after I had consigned the manuscript to my private papers.

THE RECOVERY OF WONDER

I would have them prosper …
… ripen into the fullness of all things
Johann Moser, *Most Ancient of All Splendors*

1

Where Are the Things of Yesteryear?

Mais où sont les neiges d'antan?
But where are the snows of yesteryear?
François Villon

Where are the songs of Spring? Ay, where are they?
Keats

I HAVE CHOSEN as my theme an uncommon story about a most common thing. Now, even in these days, every story needs some kind of a hero, and the hero of this story is that most homely of words and realities, the *ordinary word "thing"* and the *familiar things themselves.* Although this seems a modest, even banal, task, hardly worth undertaking, it proves to be daunting. We are so surrounded by things that the effort to look at ordinary things closely is not unlike a fish trying to understand what is meant by water: for the fish, water; for us, things.[1] They are so much with us that we are accustomed to take the way they are present to us for granted; in Wordsworth's words:

The world is too much with us; late and soon,
Getting and spending we lay waste our powers:
Little we see in Nature ... / It moves us not.

The Czech novelist Milan Kundera argues[2] that, whereas philosophers such as Husserl and Heidegger have lamented the loss of the sense of being, modern novelists, from Cervantes on, have recuperated

1 "He could understand the things at home./ And being up high had helped him when up high,/ As if on a taller tower/ He would be certain to see/ That, in the shadowless atmosphere,/ The knowledge of things lay round but unperceived ..." Wallace Stevens, *Things of August,* in *The Collected Poems of Wallace Stevens* (1954; repr. New York: Vintage 1990), 493.

2 *The Art of the Novel* (1986; repr. New York: Harper and Row 1988), 3–20.

the recent sense of things, more and more rendering them into their everyday sense. He argues that the tradition of the modern novel has moved steadily from the high romance of *Don Quixote* in the sixteenth century through the domestic letters of Richardson's *Pamela* in the eighteenth and, in the nineteenth, towards the depiction of the most mundane and ordinary things such as the prosaic daydreams of Flaubert's *Madame Bovary*, only to pass on in the twentieth to the ambiguities of Kafka's *K* and finally to the little absurdities of Hasek's *The Good Soldier Schweik*. All of this, Kundera claims, is part of the de-escalating history of being traced by the modern novel as it moves – though he is too modest to say it – towards *The Unbearable Lightness of Being*.[3]

But, even if Kundera's description of the actual history of the novel is correct, we can still ask whether it is inevitable that what the poet Wallace Stevens has called "the plain sense of things"[4] needs to be "unbearably light?" The English ordinary language philosophers – I think particularly of Austin[5] – have visited the issue before me, though the path I will follow attends more to things than to the use of words. In any event, in this most democratic of ages, why should philosophy not follow suit and probe into the most oft-repeated of ordinary meanings and realities? What is more appropriate in this age, which has been called "the age of the common man," than to unfold the narrative of the common thing?

For you and I use the word "thing" a hundred times a day and more to refer to a hundred and more very different matters. But, given my intention to pay such attention to so obvious a subject, I should not fault anyone for thinking that I had something more special in mind, even something spectacular if not so peculiar as the rather formless, sickly green image that introduces the midnight horror movie, followed by

3 The title of his own novel (1984; repr. Harper Perennial 1991). In *The Art of the Novel* (164–5), beginning with the "depreciated legacy of Cervantes," Kundera ends the volume with this observation: "For if European culture seems under threat today, if the threat from within and without hangs over what is most precious about it – its respect for the individual, for his original thought, and for his right to an inviolable private life – then, I believe, that precious essence of the European spirit is being held safe as in a treasure chest inside the history of the novel." What is absent here is the recognition that the value of the individual human being is ineluctably connected to the value we acknowledge in things.

4 *Collected Poems*, 502.

5 For example, J.O. Urmson, ed., *How to Do Things with Words*, (Oxford, U.K.: Galaxy 1965). Ordinary language philosophy is a movement associated with Ludwig Wittgenstein (1859–1951), the Austrian-born British philosopher Gilbert Ryle (1900–76), and others, who examined the meaning of words as they are used in ordinary linguistic practice. See *The Cambridge Dictionary of Philosophy*, 2nd ed. (Cambridge, U.K.: Cambridge University Press 1995; repr. 2001), 635.

the caption "The Thing from Outer Space" or "The Thing that Ate New York." But I assure you that I mean what the poet means when he says:

> After the leaves have fallen, we return
> To a plain sense of things

if only to see whether they are as plain as they are alleged to be. In addition to the difficulties of exploring such an obvious and seemingly banal topic, I must face two further difficulties. First of all, it is necessary to weigh in a bit more on the side of the history of metaphysics than would have seemed appropriate to the philosopher whose name this distinguished series bears.[6] In this, I face a dilemma not unlike that of the Renaissance Spanish humanist Juan Luis Vives. He was a vigorous opponent of St Thomas Aquinas and, upon being invited to deliver an encomium on the feast day of the saint whose views he opposed, he confessed that he found himself on a slippery slope. Was he to speak in agreement with the saint whom the occasion was meant to honour? But then he would be devious. Or should he speak his own mind? But then he would seem ungracious. So, too, I find that there is no way out of this dilemma, only the choice of one of its horns, and that the sharper. The second difficulty compounds the first. For I had started out, and still persist, in telling the remarkable story of the humble thing: the tree in the garden, the rock on the path, the puppy fawning in one's lap, the stars in the heavens and the birds on the wing. These are some of the "unmakeable things" that surround us; that is, unlike books and machines and meals, they are things not made by us.[7] I intend, therefore, to trace the quixotic history of these "unmakeables" through the Greek, medieval, modern, and contemporary periods, in order to discover the composite texture of their "unmakeability."

6 These reflections, here extensively revised, were originally offered as the 1997 Gilbert Ryle Lectures at Trent University, Peterborough, Ontario.

7 Indeed, even in the aforementioned things made by us, we do not make *everything* in them, not even in the new experiments in genetic engineering. We are not creators *ex nihilo*; our making is limited by what is given prior to our making, even when we synthesize the immediate elements of our composition. There is an oft-told joke about some magician scientists who dismissed God on the grounds that they could create whatever they wished without his aid. At that point, the story goes, God intervened and challenged them: "Show me!" They replied: "We take some dirt and ... " But at that point God intervened again, saying: "No! No! You must bring your own dirt." We are composers not creators. There is a certain ambiguity in the relation between ordinary things and their components which by extension may be called things. I have in mind, however, not simply the elements that are present in things, but also and principally the richer, complex ordinary things themselves.

But it is no secret that, since the philosophers tossed out the four causes of Aristotle in the seventeenth century, things as such have absented themselves from the mainstream of modern thought, and from respectable intellectual conversation, as though pouting over their unmerited dismissal. In modern times, things seem to have lost their substance in reality, their significance in modern scientific and intellectual discourse, and their credit in modern minds. In the argot of current political speech, they have been marginalized. They have been reduced to mere devices of unlearned common sense, good enough for butchers and bakers but not fit to be named in the learned halls of academic dons. For we may think that we still *believe* in such things, until we start to talk "scientifically," "rigorously," or even "learnedly" about them, and then instead of talking of things we talk of particles and processes, of systems and laws. This talk stands in contrast to ages past, when the notion of "thing" and the realities themselves played a prominent role in what was taken then as rigorous, intellectual, and learned discourse, that is, in philosophy and in what passed for science. Hence the title of this chapter: "Where are the things of yesteryear?"

Among others, the influential Sir Bertrand Russell sealed the fate of things, driving them into exile as mere temporary constructions of the mind, nothing more than passing thoughts or momentary linguistic events. In *Our Knowledge of the External World*[8] Lord Russell pronounced the insubstantiality of things with this dismissal:[9]

> We can now define the momentary common-sense "thing" [Russell is talking about the word], as opposed to its momentary appearances [the sensations or perceptions]. By the similarity of neighbouring perspectives [our points of view], many objects in the one [set] can be correlated with objects in the other [set], namely with the similar objects. Given an object correlated with it in all perspectives that system may be identified with the momentary common sense "thing." Thus an aspect of a "thing" is a member of the system of aspects which is the "thing" at the moment ... All the aspects of a thing are real, *whereas the thing is a merely logical construction.* It has, however, the merit of being neutral as between different points of view ...

8 Originally published in 1914. Repr. London: George Allen and Unwin 1972. The material quoted appeard on p. 96.

9 Quoted with perceptive commentary by Arthur Quinn, *The Confidence of British Philosophers* (Leiden: Brill 1977), 240.

phenomenology – return to the things themselves (Husserl + Aquinas)

We are told, then, that aspects are *real,* whereas the "thing" is merely *mental,* a construction for the convenience of the mind.

Two years earlier, in *The Problems of Philosophy* (1912),[10] Russell had put the matter still more dramatically: "The process of sound philosophizing, to my mind, consists mainly in passing from those obvious, vague, ambiguous things that we feel quite sure of to something precise, clear, definite, which by reflection and analysis we find is involved in the vague thing that we start from and is, so to speak, the real truth of which the vague thing is a sort of shadow." It will be my argument that this withdrawal of the term "thing" from its rightful place in learned discourse and in reality simply will not do.[11] Such a notion of the thing is too "thin" and too mind-dependent. But the alternative – to rescue the thing in its "thick" sense and in its full-bodied reality – is far from easy.

For there is a great variety of contexts in which we use the word. There can be no doubt that the word "thing" often functions as a placeholder for very *unthingly* things. A glance at any collection of quotable sayings will provide examples. The word may stand in for an insubstantial spirit; thus, speaking of an apparition, Bernardo whispers to Horatio: "What! has this *thing* appear'd again tonight?" Or it may serve to denote a dramatic performance; thus Hamlet plots: "The play's the *thing* wherein I'll catch the conscience of the king." Sometimes the word stands in for great events; recalling his close victory over Napoleon, Wellington – thinking no doubt of the belated arrival of Blucher – remarked: "It has been a damned nice *thing,* the nearest run *thing* you ever saw in your life." And, in more modest yet general vein, those who do not have to face such great events as the Battle of Waterloo may yet complain that "life is just one damned *thing* after another." Sometimes the word is used of ideas and propositions; Browning complained of a good bishop that "he said true *things,* but called them by wrong names." And Gilbert's pungent line suggests their untrustworthiness: "*Things* are seldom what they seem, Skim milk masquerades as cream." Or the word

10 Quoted in Trent University, *Prospectus and Honour Brochure* (Department of Philosophy 1991–92), 4.

11 Russell went through a number of stages in his philosophy; see *My Philosophical Development* (London: George Allen and Unwin 1959); *The Autobiography of Bertrand Russell* (New York: Simon and Schuster 1967–69), 3 vols.; and *My Own Philosophy* (Hamilton, Ont.: McMaster University 1972). Russell did maintain the legitimacy of common-sense language alongside that of logical construction; but it was for the sake of utility rather than for exactness of thought or intelligible insight.

may even stand in for non-existent objects, as when Shakespeare laments: "O hateful error, melancholy's child/ Why dost thou show, to the apt thoughts of men,/ The *things* that are not?"

And, even more indeterminately, we often use the word in an empty sort of way, intending to fill it in with a more particular description. "Get me that *thing-um-a-gig* over there, will you please? ... I mean that *thing* on the bench ... You know! (and finally, in exasperation over our own inarticulateness and the perplexity of our helper) – the hammer." With so many diverse referents, ranging from ghosts to imaginings to propositions to non-existents to empty categories, the word seems to be a mere place-holder that invites the dismissal it receives from Russell. For it seems to mean anything and everything and in substance nothing, or at least nothing very much, being little more than a convenient mental peg on which to hang our vagueness and our fancies.

And so, given such a bewildering plethora of varied uses, it is perhaps not surprising that Lord Russell should banish it from enlightened speech. But if aspects are real, why not things, too? Is there perhaps a strong and privileged sense of the word, a principal meaning, a paradigmatic sense that is the prince among the many uses of the word? A presidential use that presides over the many meanings and that refers us to a reality which commands the original and primary sense and which is resident in and disclosed through the word? Might there not be, so to speak, a chairman of the board of many uses?

I take my first clue from an old refrain, which at first glance does not seem to augur well for the enterprise of reclaiming the *real* sense of things, for it thrums its lines thus:

> You're nothing but a nothing, a rum thing, a dumb thing, You're nothing but a nothing – you're not a thing at all!

I take some small consolation and a hint from the concession in the last line, which draws no more than a diaphanous membrane between a thing and whatever is not a thing: you're not a *thing* at all! For at least that tells us that the object of denial and contempt in the song is thereby identified in opposition to whatever is a thing:

> You're nothing but a nothing – you're *not* a thing at all.

This is slim pickings, to be sure; but it is a beginning, and every journey must begin with a single step and every story with a single word. May we assume, then, that the word "thing" has at least some consistency, enough to distinguish it ever so slightly – yet definitively – from "nothing"? At least it must be conceded that, judging by the frequency with which we use the word to refer to something or other, the word clings to tongue and mind with the consistency of sticky putty. At the very least, what it refers to is not nothing; indeed, we use it on almost every occasion, for each and every thing. Could we ever do without the word?

In desperation I turned to that familiar old warhorse, the English equivalent of the Académie française: I mean the *Oxford English Dictionary,* known affectionately as the *OED*. It documents two senses of the word "thing". It tells us that the *emphatic* meaning of the word "thing" is whatever is distinguished from the totality of being – the all in all – on the one hand, and the attributes of individuals – their colours, shapes, and sounds – on the other. The same arbiter of proper English also lists another meaning of the word, something rather different from the emphatic thing sandwiched between the universe, on the one hand, and the attributes of individuals, on the other. For it tells us that the original meaning of the word "thing" is that of an *assembly,* a public meeting of some moment.

It is important to notice this last qualification: for in the assembly, supposedly, matters of considerable public importance are deliberated and acted upon with authority. It is the weightiness in this second meaning that links the word with the Latin derivatives, the French *chose* and the Italian *cosa,* both derived from the Latin *causa*; and from which we in turn derive the word "case," as in "court case". Some philosophers, notably Martin Heidegger, have made much of this meaning, taking the word to designate the coalescence of hidden forces.[12]

Dare we associate the two meanings? Dare we take from this double sense, and from the variety of uses, one significant fact: in contrast to its apparent commonness, its meanness and lowliness, its profligacy, the word "thing" often carries with it a certain self-assertiveness, a certain consistency and weight (according to the emphatic meaning), and also a certain importance and value (implied in the assembly meaning). Is it the case that the insistent core which is central to the *emphatic* meaning of the word suggests something of import and value as well? Might it be, then, that the emphatic meaning of the word, which refers to that which is sandwiched between the totality of the universe (all being) and the

12 The close neighbour of the term in German, however, is the word *Sache,* which is often, though not precisely, used as synonymous with the word *Ding.* Perhaps the closest expression of this meaning is the English "state of affairs," though, in the hands of many linguistic philosophers, that term is loaded with philosophical presuppositions of an empiricist and positivist sort.

attributes of individuals, deserves a place in discourse about reality after all? My chief concern, at the moment, is to suggest that the emphatic sense of the word discloses enough weight to merit its referent being the hero of this story. For the story is both a comedy and a tragedy, a tragic-comical adventure that will take us back through our own cultural memories, back to the ancient Greeks, through the Middle Ages, to the modern period and even beyond it to our present intellectual milieu.

Such a journey calls upon us to move beyond the general and relatively empty sense already remarked upon, the sort of verbal chameleon that can take on the colour of different objects and situations; or rather that can bleach that colour out, and that can stand for real or imagined unities of meaning – in a word, for anything that has enough consistency of meaning to hold the mind's attention. My attention, however, will be directed principally to a second, more realistic sense, which melds the two meanings documented by the *OED*, the core meaning and the value meaning. This requires us to consider the more concrete referents, the *emphatic* sense once we attribute to it something of an as yet undefined import. And so we return to what I have called our quite ordinary and instinctive sense of things: the things of nature – trees, grass, animals, the birds of the sky and the fishes of the sea.

To repeat: we often call something a "thing" because we have in mind no better, no more precise word for it; we use the word as a verbal placeholder. This might be called a "thin" sense of the word. But I will argue that the weight inherent in the consistency of the word links the core meaning with the assembly meaning in such as way as to suggest that even the relatively empty sense is grounded in the principal, the emphatic sense of the term. It is this "thick" sense that discloses a unity of no small significance.

In conceding that it is not easy to retrieve the richer sense of the word "thing", I am conscious that I have yet to show convincing grounds why the journey is worth setting out upon. It may yet seem to fall victim to the strictures which the philosopher Thomas Hobbes put upon such subtleties – namely, that they are not worth the labour expended upon them, and that they will prove to be barren, producing but a few useless acorns instead of copious fruits and crops.[13] Lest what follows seems to be remote and empty speculation, I propose that a proper understanding of what the word "thing" offers to reflection lights up the horizon of our understanding and has a direct impact upon our *freedom*; so that a proper understanding of the nature and status of things through reflection upon the emphatic meaning of the word is a matter of import for each and all of us.

13 *De corpore* I, 1.

The link between our freedom and the recovery of a strong sense of things, a "thick" sense, requires also the recovery of *wonder*; and, if we take our cue from Aristotle, this *is* the proper business of philosophy, for he acknowledged that philosophy begins just there – in wonder. Wonder is the middle term that joins our freedom to the dignity of things. For it will be the thesis of my argument that human freedom increases, not insofar as we subjugate things, but insofar as we give them their due. These reflections, then, are offered as a work of intellectual justice, and are meant to bear upon the way we approach our environment with a deeper sense of its ecological importance. It is difficult, however, to take the notion of "thing" seriously. It is so available: as we have seen, we use it to refer to physical realities but also to imaginary ones, to memories and wishes, to artifacts and futurables, to images and dreams, to plans and plays, and even, in the last resort, to "things that are not." Indeed, we use it for everything that is or is not a silly thing, a dumb thing, a nothing but a nothing.

But there is an even more pressing difficulty which I have already touched upon and to which I now return. Would I be far wrong were I to suggest that our modern intellectual culture convinces us that we ought not to really *believe* in things anymore? Or at least, that our intellectual culture discourages such "primitive" belief? I must explain myself. You and I handle things as we make our daily rounds, and we may respond to things with feeling and imagination as we read the poets. But we do not *think* things, that is, with scientific or intellectual rigour. We do not let things enter into the "serious" passes of our minds. As evidence of this, I offer the following reflection. Initiated into modern culture, if we were asked to give a rational account of some thing such as the tree in the garden, I suspect that we would first of all describe a set of colours and shapes, its bark rough or smooth; well enough! But if we were pressed to penetrate more deeply to its "real constitution" in an effort to understand the make-up of the tree and to give a "rationally coherent account" of it – would not the tree as a *thing* dissolve into a cloud of particles and processes, of cellular structures and photosyntheses? For we are taught to think that there are particles, waves, and processes governed by systemic laws, but not *things.*

Is the *tree*, then, more than a collection? That is, has it – in the words of the OED – an *emphatic* reality and not just an emphatic meaning? Or is this just an illusion of our errant common sense? a shadowy cloud that evaporates before the bright light of the mind? Are there things "between" the totality of all being and the collection of cells and processes? Or is the very notion of *thing* like a category mistake? Professor Ryle's famous anecdote comes to mind about the visitor who wished to see Oxford University. After being shown the various colleges – Trinity,

Magdalen, and the others – the visitor then asked to see the university. Is the word "thing" like that, not so much a mental convenience as a category mistake?[14] Is it that, after hearing the account of the cellular structures and the processes, we still ask mistakenly and redundantly for an account of the tree as such, as the visitor had asked to see the university after having seen its colleges? We ought to be careful before we answer, for if we persist in asking for an intellectual account of the tree in terms other than cellular structures and processes, we will have fallen – perhaps unintentionally, even unwillingly – into the pit of metaphysics, unless we have the imagination and good fortune to fall onto the pad of poetry. And yet, is it possible that, while we may have forgotten the sense of things, "Nature yet remembers/ What was so fugitive?"

A poet can provoke wonder under the spell of things. For the poets do very well with ordinary things. Wallace Stevens entitles a poem "Not Ideas about the Thing, but the Thing Itself."[15] And Rupert Brooke celebrates them in *The Great Lover*:

> Shall I not crown them with immortal praise
> Whom I have loved … These I have loved:
> … the blue bitter smoke of wood;
> And radiant raindrops couching in cool flowers;
> And flowers themselves, that sway through sunny hours,
> Dreaming of moths that drink them under the moon; …
> Dear
> names,
> And thousand others throng to me! …
> And oaks; and brown horse-chestnuts, glossy-new;
> And new-peeled sticks; and shining pools on grass; –
> All these have been my loves.

And then, breaking the hymnody of praise, with shock at the fragility of these same things, which the poet suffers as a betrayal, he mourns:

> And these shall pass …
> Nor all my passion, all my prayers, have power
> To hold them with me through the gate of Death.

14 In the *Science of Logic* (preface to the 2nd ed.; trans. A.V. Miller, New York: Humanities Press 1969, 41), Hegel makes a somewhat comparable remark: "The uncouth and uneducated behaviour of taking a category which is under consideration for *something other* than the category itself." And earlier still, Aristotle had already criticized *metabasis eis allo genos.*

15 *Collected Poems,* 534.

Only memory can hold things for a short while in its feeble grasp. But where are the things of yesteryear?

And so I set sail for ancient Greece in search of the things of yesteryear, hoping to find there the things that now live on the periphery of our consciousness and dress themselves in the modern-day tatters of common sense. I was surprised, however, that I did not quite find in the earlier philosophers what I had expected to find, the familiar notion of the thing so commonly voiced in our English language. Instead, I found the faceless demonstrative pronoun "those" (*ta tauta*), without a noun to fill out the pronoun with more determinate content. And even less definite still, simply the indiscriminate "all" (*ta panta*), as in the famous saying attributed by later writers to Heraclitus that "all is in flux: *panta rhei.*"

Or again, I found *ta pragmata* and *ta chrêmata*, literally, what is at hand and what is useable. The word "thing" that we find in English translations of the Greek texts either is not present in the early Greek writings or is expressed with words belonging to the field of utility or action. In the main, the early Greek thinkers used these two words for what we translate as "thing", namely, *chrêma* and *pragma*, usually in their plural forms: *ta chrêmata* and *ta pragmata*. Because the Greeks filled their language with value, however, *chrêma* does not refer to a thing without qualification, rather, it refers to what is useful, not in the modern technological sense of utility, but to a worthwhile thing capable of realizing not only the human good but the good of the cosmos as well. *Chrêma* derives from a word that can mean the serviceability of a thing, something one needs such as money, property, wealth, or goods, but it is also often associated with an endowment from the gods.[16] The word *pragma*, on the other hand, signifies action, a deed, that which is done, something achieved, and in the plural (*ta pragmata*) it can signify private or public affairs. It thus approaches the sense of "assembly" previously noticed. *Pragma* is closely related to *praxis*, a transaction, derived from *prassô*, which means to bring something about by action, to carry out a practical activity. In sum, then, we have among the early Greeks the notions of serviceability and practicability in place of what is often translated into English as "thing".

not utility but realizing a good.

This lexicon does not seem to provide us with the grounds for the high metaphysics of Plato and Aristotle. There can be no doubt that the

16 *Chrêma* becomes the most general word for "thing". Anaxagoras is the first philosopher to use it in the sense of "thing," though it probably held this sense in the sixth century BC (Fragment B 1; H. Diels, *Die Fragmente der Vorsokratiker* 6th ed., edited by W. Kranz [Berlin: Weidmann, 1951], vol. 2. The ancient root *chrê* carries with it the sense of necessity as that which is proper, appropriate, fitting. I am indebted to Kurt Pritzl, OP, for a helpful discussion of this usage.

early Greek philosophers sought the origin (*archê, archai*) of all things, but they paid attention more to the universe as a whole. They consistently used the terms in the plural, not so much in the sense of a collection of individuals as in the sense of the ordered whole. They grasped the universe as a cosmos. Anaximander, the associate of the first recorded philosopher, Thales, already in the middle of the sixth century BCE, had the elements of the notion of an orderly arrangement of things, governed by what he called justice (*dikê*), a justice that pronounced the fate not only of men but of things; that is, *dikê* is not simply a human ethical justice but a cosmic one as well.

It may have been his successor, Anaximenes, who first made philosophical use of the word "cosmos" (*kosmos*).[17] In any event, there can be no doubt that the notion of the *kosmos* is present to the minds of these early Greek thinkers. Empedocles, in the middle of the fifth century BCE, said that mind (*nous*) held the *kosmos* together in unity (Fr. 134). A little later, we find Democritus comparing man to the *kosmos* as a little cosmos (*mikrokosmos*). The Pythagoreans found the unifying principle of the *kosmos* in number and measure (*arithmos*), though, once again, not in our putative value-neutral modern sense, but in the sense that contributed to the beauty and the goodness of the whole. Thus, the sexual myths of origin had given way in the earliest philosophers to an ethical-cosmic sense of order which, still with a sense of value,[18] could be expressed in terms of a mathematical and ethical symbolism of order.

This sense of an intrinsically ordered whole, a cosmos as distinct from a chaos, received its canonical status in the culture with the great tragedies, especially those of Aeschylus, whose Prometheus defiantly trumpets his discovery of the universe as ordered rightly from within itself.[19] It is important to notice that, for both the poet and the philosopher, *kosmos* is not simply a descriptive term but a normative one as well. It is this normative sense of necessity that is operative in Parmenides's great poem, so that the concept of method (*met'hodos*) is not simply a mental exercise but a way of life seeking the human and the universal good.

17 Although such a claim must be qualified by a quite general difficulty. For this particular claim is based upon a doxographer writing two centuries later, and who (like other later writers, such as Aristotle and Simplicius) may have substituted their later technical vocabulary for the original.

18 I use the term without its Kantian association with human evaluation, but rather to designate the good present within a thing and within the cosmos.

19 *Prometheus*, P. V, l, 459. Cf. W. Jaeger, *Paideia: The Ideals of Greek Culture*, 3 vols., 2nd ed. (1945; repr. Oxford, U.K.: Galaxy 1965), 1: 164.

We need to carry this normative sense of necessity forward with us as we approach the high metaphysics of Plato and Aristotle; for with them we find the notion of "things" (*chrêmata* and *pragmata*) translated into the vocabulary of *being*: *ta onta,* no longer merely the things that are serviceable or actionable; but *simpliciter,* the things that *are.* It is not easy for us to recapture the breathtaking shift of horizon entailed by this translation. This radical transformation at once carried forward the still somewhat poetic concept of the good as *dikê* while it absolutized the horizon of dikê and invested it with a value-laden transcendental quality. With these new philosophers, who followed upon Parmenides's radical and uncompromising break with the *physikoi,* an absolute sense of being as such permeated the field of philosophy and defined the horizon of its concern, indeed for the next two millenia. Being (*on, ousia*) is not, then, a mere fact of existence. Plato underscores this when he remarks that "you should also say that not only do the objects of knowledge owe their *being known* to the good, but their *being* is also due to it."[20] Even with Aristotle, the good is present throughout the cosmos, manifesting itself in a variety of analogous *ends (teloi)* appropriate to the nature of each being. The earlier philosophers had occasionally used the term in the plural (*ta onta*) but without preferring it to others. Heidegger quite rightly has found this metaphysical translation into being (*Sein, das Seiende*) fateful for Western culture,[21] but I will take a different path in unfolding the story of the thing.

It is fruitful, I think, to look at a remarkable development in Greek culture, society, and thought that rested upon two significant events in the eighth century BCE: first, the move to literacy through the development of a Greek written alphabet, adapted from the Phoenicians; and second, the formation of that unique Greek institution, the *polis.* We translate this latter institution with the English term "city-state," but, in fact, the

20 *Republic* 509b; to which he adds: "although the good is not being, but superior to it in rank and power." My emphasis.

21 See, for example, *Vom Wesen der Wahrheit,* 4th ed. (Frankfurt: Vittorio Klostermann 1961) or *Platons Lehre von der Wahrheit mit einen Brief über den "Humanismus" 2nd ed. (Bern:* Francke Verlaq 1954). In *Die Frage nach dem Ding* (Tübingen: Max Niemeyer 1962; English translation, *What Is a Thing?* [Chicago: Regnery/Gateway 1967], G53-4/E70), Heidegger lists several meanings of thing: *ta physika,* "things insofar as they originate and come forth from themselves"; *ta poioumena,* "things insofar as they are produced by the human hand"; *ta chrêmata,* "things insofar as they are in use and therefore stand at our constant disposal"; *ta pragmata,* "things insofar as we have to do with them at all"; and finally, *ta mathêmata,* which becomes the principal sense (*mathêsis universalis*) that Heidegger examines in the rest of this work, stressing above all the *Vorverständnisse* (pre-understandings) that we bring to our understanding of things.

polis is neither a city in the sense of a modern metropolis nor a state in the sense of a modern nation. Among its other services, the *polis* was a place of meeting, of barter, and, even before Socrates, of conversation; in a word, the Greek *agora* or market was a place for the exchange of goods and ideas. Later, in the fifth and fourth centuries BCE, it was intellectually alive, brilliantly but not exclusively in Athens. The enterprise of recovering a strong sense of things can be furthered by tracing the intellectual development that flowed from this special time and place.

Hegel remarks upon a decisive cultural shift that occurred among the Greeks. They "objectified" themselves, he tells us. Yet they did so, not in our alledgedly value-neutral sense of objectivity, but with the impassioned value-laden projection of themselves as a people within the mirror of the world; so that the world reflected their own deeds not simply subjectively as actions but objectively as *events*. In this way they came to understand themselves as a people distinct from others. This way of understanding is so familiar to us, who are heirs of the Greeks, that it is difficult to appreciate the shift in consciousness brought about by such self-distantcing. Werner Jaeger is not afraid to call it a new conception of truth.[22] And so the ill-suited term "distantiation," can be more accurately described as a "liberation" from the immediate confinement of their situation. Moreover, as I will argue later, the constancy of the fascination the Greeks work upon us indicates that, paradoxically, that "distantiation" is a new way of entering more deeply into the reality of the cosmos.

The teacher who introduced me to philosophy in a formal way, Father Henry Carr, CSB, used to startle his classes by proclaiming that "only the Greeks had a grammar." Immediately objections would be voiced to the effect that in every language group there are speakers of great eloquence. He would shake his head and reply that he was speaking not of the eloquent use of language but of quite another matter. He did not elaborate his assertion in any detail, thinking it sufficient to provoke philosophical neophytes to reflection. And, indeed, over the years I have been provoked into developing his suggestive remark.

Of course, grammar may help in the accurate use of language, but it is not identical with its skilful and eloquent practice; its genius lies elsewhere. For with the discovery of grammar, the Greeks, by an effort of mind and imagination, withdrew partially from the immediacy of their

22 "Yet in this victory of the rational *I* over traditional authority, there is latent a force which is to triumph over the individual: the concept of Truth, a new universal category to which every personal preference must yield" (Jaeger, *Paideia*, 1:155). And, reflecting upon Socrates and Plato, he speaks of "a new form of knowledge" (*ibid.* 2:168).

spoken language in order to lay it out before themselves and to dissect or analyse its functional elements: eventually into nouns, verbs, adjectives, adverbs, prepositions, moods, conjugations, and declensions.[23] The Greeks "distanced" themselves from their language in order to understand how and why the language functioned as it did; in this sense, they "objectified" it. The earliest known monuments of grammar go back no farther than the middle of the fifth century BCE to Prodicus, but the analysis itself must have gone on for some time before. As it developed, this effort became the study of the use of language in what today we call – using a Greek name – the *organon*, which includes logic, the study of basic categories and propositions, the analytics of proof, and the study of topics and sophistic fallacies. To this list, if instead of the modern Aristotelian canon (as published by Bekker in the nineteeth century) we were to use the Arabic *organon*, we might add the Poetics and the Rhetoric, indicating a somewhat different conception of learned language. Today, we could gather all of these studies under the umbrella term "language studies," which was eventually in our own era to include modern linguistics.

But there were other paths opened up by "objectification" in the sense of "distantiation", and it is important to consider them briefly because each path opens up a new aspect in the search for the truth of what we call "things". By a second path, those whom today we call philosophers asked about the primordial character of things and cosmos, and sought to distinguish such an account from prior myths. Along yet a third path of enquiry, the Pythagoreans sought for the unity of all things in number, as among the Greeks mathematics came to be a science distinct from practical engineering. Finally, especially with Herodotus and Thucydides, history found its tongue in seeking out the worthwhile reasons (*aitiai*) to account for the deeds of men and the events of their history.

In their essentials, then, we find four primary disciplines among the Greeks, that is, four distinctive ways of talking about things.[24] They are four fundamental modes of discourse, four basic ways of giving a rational account of things, four paths to understanding them. They are not, of

4 ways

23 It comes as a surprise to those of us who have been taught grammar in a more or less systematic, non-historical manner to realize how long the development of such distinctions took, some being formulated only in relatively recent times. See any good history of grammar, or, from a postmodern linguistic point of view, Julia Kristeva, *Language the Unknown* (1981; repr. New York: Columbia 1989), especially chapter 16, "The Grammar of Port-Royal."

24 I say "distinctive" because, while they can be – and have been – combined with one another to form hybrid accounts during the course of later Western cultures, these paths are so elemental that they have not been – and cannot be – confused with one another.

course, the only modes of expression, but they are the only *cognitive* modes (as distinct from, for example, symbolic or imaginative modes), that is, the only conceptual, methodical, explanatory modes. In order to describe these modes, it will be clearer if a later, more developed and stable terminology is used to describe them, rather than the variable terminology of the earliest Greek thinkers. Let me name them, then, and characterize them somewhat anachronistically in the profile by which we recognize them today, as they have been applied to the study of the cosmos.[25]

First, there is *philosophy*, by which everything is translated into fundamental categories of origin (*archai*), whether it be water, air, fire, atoms, or being. The latter eventually won out over against other contenders, undoubtedly because of its absolutely comprehensive and primordial character.[26] Secondly, there is *mathematics*, the rational account of things in terms of their numerical and, in some cases, measurable relations. As

25 The terminology among the early Greek thinkers was not stable, so that it took some time before the original conceptual temper of each mode became clearly distinct. Thus, it took a considerable time for mathematics to restrict itself from the more general sense of a learned method (*mathesis universalis*) to the science of numerically defined relations. Indeed, in the High Middle Ages, it still designated a study of concepts broad enough to include abstract qualities (for example, *albedo*) in contrast to concrete substances. Or to take a second example, the original empirical studies of nature, which we today identify as the fragments of the "philosophers", often bore the name *istoriê*, without the restriction to our own sense of history as the rational account of temporally ordered events. Some residue of that usage comes to us in the older term "natural history", which need not have a strict connection with time. Nevertheless, though the terminology wavered, the essential lines of the approaches themselves are already discernible in the Greek names they have borne in their long careers; and their proper character can be discerned within the ancient usage. For a somewhat more detailed consideration, see my essay "Are There Things More Important for the Human Race Than Survival? The Greek Heritage: Rationality," in N. Lobkowicz and Hanns Martin Schleyer-Stiftung, ed., *Das europäische Erbe und seine christliche Zukunft* (Köln: Backem 1985), 348ff. (German version: 95ff.).

26 Cf. the comparative linguistic studies in the volumes on the verb "to be" in Morris Halle and Benson Mates, ed., *Foundations of Language: Supplementary Series* (Dordrecht: Reidel). Of especial interest are the volumes by Charles H. Kahn on ancient Greek and James Barr on biblical Hebrew and biblical Greek. Charles Ferguson (vol. 14, ed. John W.M. Verhaar [1972] 78–9) points out that "every language has at least one set of forms or constructions whose primary function ... is to denote existence ... in the limiting case [to denote] existence apart from specific location. In other words, every language has an existential element such as a verb or particle, and the denotation of existence is never merely a marginal function of something else." Similarly, every language has at least one set of forms to designate copulative relationships. In the same volume Peri Bhaskararao's study of the Dravidian Telugu leads him to underline "the absolute necessity of the verb 'to be' at the base level" (204–5). The development by which *ta onta* came to such primacy in Plato and Aristotle is the more exceptional given the ambiguity that surrounds the Greek terms *on*, *einai*

this study sought its own genius, it was to detach itself from interpretation of the cosmos to become a study on its own terms, specifically, a study of relations to which a numerical value can be assigned. Thirdly, *history* was to become the rational study of human action and subsequently of temporal relations in an objectified context, that is, as an account in terms of events. Fourthly, we have already seen, in the remarks about the study of grammar, the seeds of what was to become the study of logic and more generally of *linguistics.*

If we scan the more than twenty-five hundred years of our indebtedness to the Greeks, we can see a certain shift of weight among these four modes, each coming into prominence during succeeding eras in Western culture. The early classical period, continuing into the Middle Ages, can be characterized as philosophical in the sense of metaphysics, the study of first principles within the interpretive horizon of *being.* The early and middle modern period, through the sixteenth to the eighteenth centuries, can be characterized as primarily *mathematical,* with its interest in formulating numerically assignable correlations. It was not until the *historical* turn towards the end of the eighteenth century, however, that history came into its own as the study of actual events understood in and through the dynamic of time; so that all subject matters – those of geology and archaeology, art, religion, science, and even mathematics itself – came to be seen to have a history. With this appreciation of the intelligible role of time, a fuller rational explanation of these

(being, to be) and *ousia* (essence). The ambiguity is compounded by the use (confined almost entirely to Indo-European languages) of the same term for the copula and for existential predication. The passage of the Greek texts through the Semitic languages of Syriac, Arabic, and Hebrew, before returning to the Indo-European languages (scholastic Latin, French, English, German, and so on), effected some clarification regarding the ambiguity of the existential and copulative uses. But it is in Arabic that the distinction is made between essence and existence most sharply and from which it came to prominence in medieval Latin (Bhaskararao, 225). These interesting observations may, on the one hand, seem to relativize the high metaphysics of Plato and Aristotle along the lines of Benjamin Whorff's thesis, but we might reflect, on the contrary, upon the remarkable emergence of the philosophy of being within such opaque and unpromising linguistic conditions. This is implied when Bhaskararao remarks that, lacking the distinction between the existential and copulative functions of *einai,* Aristotle is "forced to go to lengths to get his meaning across: he does not mean '*to be this or that*' but '*simply to be absolutely*'" (226–7). Cf. also, on the same development, the progression cited by St Thomas Aquinas, *Summa theologiae* I, 44, 2, in which, following Aristotle but going beyond him with Avicenna (Ibn Sina), he traces the march of the understanding from sensible images (among the pre-Socratics) to being understood as type (*eidos*: Plato and Aristotle) to the understanding of being *simpliciter,* that is, absolutely and as such (*quidam,* but understanding Avicenna and himself).

fields required an account of their historical development. Everything was seen to have a history and to be fully explained only in and through that history. Finally, there is the study of language (logic and its affiliates), which has blossomed with new life in our own century, in what Richard Rorty has called "the *linguistic* turn."

In subsequent developments within the cultures influenced by the Greeks, including our own, these four modes often mingled to form hybrid accounts, but it is significant that (except for linguistics) they have kept their original Greek names: logic, mathematics, history, and philosophy, all arising out of – or at least, along with – that intellectual shift that we find in grammar. From this intellectual revolution there followed, by extension and transformation, innumerable studies such as philology, hermeneutics, phenomenology, physics, psychology, and metaphysics – all held to their essential character by their Greek names and inspired by the Greek approach to their subject matter. A key concept, expressing their essential character, underlies each of the four original modes of discourse: in philosophy, *being*; in mathematics, *number*; in history, *time*; and in linguistics, the *word*, as each account struggles to release its own genius. As far as I can tell, we have used one of these four modes of discourse or a hybrid of them *and none other* in order to give rational theoretical accounts of the things that are.[27]

It is not easy to appreciate what has gone on in this ancient revolution. I have already mentioned the shift by which the Greeks objectified their actions, turning them into events in the world and thus "objectifying" the flow of time, and also how they "objectified" their language. Instead of "objectification," which carries anachronistic and misleading modern associations, I have used the word "distantiation," for the Greek "distanced" himself partially from the immediacy of his actions and his surroundings. I say, "partial distantiation," because the Greek did not flee the world, but rather, by a partial "liberation" from the immediacy and particularity of his situation, he was able to penetrate it more deeply, immerse himself more profoundly, engage himself more passionately in the situation in which he found himself. The central means to this liberation was "concept-formation." I do not mean that, before this revolution of the mind, the Greeks were without ideas, or that other

27 I am not sure why this is so. It seems that these four features – being, number, time, and word – are basic to the subject matter of rational enquiry as well as resonating with the structure of the cosmos. Of course, they do not exhaust the ways in which human intelligence is exercised; however, they reveal how, in the intellectual traditions stemming from the Greeks, we have given form to our rational theoretical accounts, explanations, and arguments.

cultures have not also found ways to articulate their understanding.[28] But the Greeks'concept-formation took shape as a partial distancing from their immediate and particular situation, their *Sitz im Leben*.

Today we may quickly convict conceptualization of being abstract and static, but such a dismissal misses the great adventure implicit in the operation of concept-formation. Admittedly, the result of conceptualization is so powerful that it may carry us, and often has, away from its own origin in the world about us and into barren speculation; but that is the corruption of its strength. In its proper and original form, it was indeed, and still can be, a liberation from the immediacy and particularity of too close an identification with locality, tribe, and era, including our own prejudices. Lodged within this operation is the very notion of universal humanity itself and of the cosmos as the totality of the things that are. It will be objected that this openness claims too much for the Greeks, who gave to others the term "babblers" (*barbaroi*), and that it neglects the often strong sense of humanity to be found in other cultures. Like us, so too the Greeks were never free of their prejudgments. Moreover, I do not mean to compare the Greek discovery with others, or to deny that some form of it is not present in other cultures.[29] It is simply that the discovery made by the Greeks stands no matter however similar discoveries there may have been in other cultures.

28 Indeed, myth and symbolism are already partial sublimations of reflective experience and may well be the necessary condition, provided in the Greek culture by the poets, for the emergence of conceptualization in the Greek manner. On conceptualization, Hans Georg Gadamer remarks: "Does not this [the development of philosophy as a science of reason] mean that thinking about what rationality, *ratio*, reason is – the very determination of these concepts themselves, the articulation of the words that designate them – constitutes already the task of philosophy? Other cultures, for example, the Chinese, have – when they have tried to retrieve by thought the fundamental questions of mankind which have been opened up by the religions – clearly taken other ways than those of science and conceptualisation. How the idea of rationality was developed in Greek thought and how 'rationality' ... has defined its place among all philosophical concepts – to ask these questions is not at all a secondary historical task – it encompasses the whole realm of the science of reason that we call philosophy, the whole realm of reason itself." ("Historical Transformations of Reason," in T. Geraets, ed., *Rationality Today/La rationalité aujourd'hui* [Ottawa: Éditions de l'université d'Ottawa 1979], 3). Obviously, "reason," in the technical sense of rendering a theoretical account, is here meant and not the whole scope of intellectual insight, which in other cultures and in our own can take other forms.

29 For example, Buddhist logics show a high degree of speculative power; and classical Indian linguistics display a marked subtlety, often making distinctions comparable with those in Western culture. See, for example, K. Kunjunni Raja, *Indian Theories of Meaning* (Madras: Adyar Centre 1963; repr. 1977).

This double discovery of distantiation and conceptualization opened the way for what we have come to call a rational account, whether in terms of reality, temporal events, numerical relations, or linguistic functions. In each of these, the path lay open to a deeper penetration of the subject matter. For the Greek mind could not be satisfied except by uncovering the necessity in things, the very necessity that had been expressed poetically and dramatically in their mythology and cosmogony by such terms as fate and destiny (*moira, anangkê, nemesis*). These necessities found dramatic expression in the tragedians, but they also found methodical expression in the approach to the world that the Greeks came to call *theôria.* This term is easily misunderstood today, for with us theory tends to mean a viewpoint brought to, if not imposed by the mind upon, the subject matter to be explained.

The term did not always carry the meaning of learned discourse. The term *theôria* comes from the Greek *theôros,* a word originally associated with the sacred, even as the Latin *contemplatio* seems associated with the temple. For the Greeks, the *theôros* was an emissary, literally, "one who sees". The root sense of the Greek word is to be found in the verb "to observe" (*theôreô*), to watch and to report, and initially under the sacred necessity to report with absolute fidelity. The word named an official delegate of a given city sent to observe the athletic games and to bring the news – of victory it was hoped – back to the *polis.* The *prophêtês* was the one who declared the message of victory at the Games, while the *theôros* witnessed the message and, returning, declared it to the public of the *polis.* We even have a reference to such "Hellenistic" practices in the Bible (2 *Maccabees* 4:18–19). Similarly, the *theôros* was the official who was delegated to bring back the message of the oracle. Such a message was a privileged communication, so that "to be a *theôros* you may not change for your audience one iota of what the god had imparted to you, just as the man who consults the oracles must report to the community exactly what the priestess had told."[30]

This strong sense of necessity was already enshrined in the Greek myths, but it became transformed in the broader notion of what the Greeks called *theôria.*[31] In Plato the initial association with religion

30 George Nagy, *Pindar's Homer* (Baltimore, Md.: Johns Hopkins University Press, 1990), 164–5.

31 See the early chapter in N. Lobkowicz, *Theory and Practice* (South Bend, Ind.: University of Notre Dame Press 1967), on the development of the idea of *theôria,* especially in Aristotle; also, Jaeger, *Paideia,* vol. 1, for the development in Plato and his predecessors. For the religious and cultural origins, see W. Kroll and K. Mittelhaus, ed., *Paulys Realencyclopädie der classischen Altertumswissenschaft,* revised by G. Wissova (Stuttgart: A. Drukenmüller 1934), 2228ff.

found expression in the openness to the divine things which call for our participation in the life of the eternal forms; so too Aristotle, for whom the highest theory was to contemplate the blessed life of the gods.

We might call Jean-Henri Fabre a modern-day *theôros*, inasmuch as he described his insects' behaviour with such loving fidelity to their daily rounds,[32] thus exemplifying the strong sense that "theory is openness to the things we have not made," the "unmakeable things." It should be said, however, that by extension the theoretical attitude can be brought to all things, including artifacts, since the emphasis of the *Bios thêoretikos* is upon fidelity to what is observed, whether made by us or not, with the recognition that even the things made by us are not made by us absolutely but contain within themselves "unmakeable," that is, unmade, constituents. Simply put, the original meaning of theory is openness to the things that are. I have emphasized "unmakeable" things because they call uncompromisingly for an open receptivity to the environment in which we find ourselves. And we should not assume that such a receptive attitude is merely passive. Gabriel Marcel, the French philosopher of the concrete, has drawn our attention to the heightened sensibility with which we must dispose ourselves in order to receive what others, including things, have to show to us.[33]

A shift of attitude is discernible at the beginnings of the modern era. The seventeenth century confirmed the shift with the genius of philosophers of such stature as Francis Bacon, René Descartes, and others. The few philosophers to whom we give the accolade "great" stand out because they are perceived to have gathered up prior trends within philosophical reflection, given them their own stamp, and shown the way to

32 *Souvenirs Entymologiques*, translated into English with the title, *The Insect World of Jean-Henri Fabre.*

33 The interventions of modern experimentation may serve a theoretical aim in "pure" science, provided that the interventions are meant eventually to lead, even if indirectly, to the observation of the things that are. Thus, models in scientific research may serve a practical purpose by enabling the technician to control a situation, or they may serve a theoretical purpose by enabling the scientist to gain a new illumination into the object of his search. Such a theoretical attitude can be subordinated to *praxis* only with risk, for the theoretical attitude tends to lose ground as the findings of science are surrendered to the practical aims and power of technology. This is even more likely to happen in the human sciences, where the contemporary sense of praxis has built into it a preference often willed without direct dependence upon theoretical observation. See Lobkowicz, *Theory and Practice*, especially the later chapters on the nineteenth century; but the whole study, including the ancient and medieval periods is, to my knowledge, the best available to the English reader.

future developments. Along with Bacon and Descartes, the writings of Spinoza and Hobbes, Leibniz and Locke are memorable and still influential for that reason. Descartes and Bacon proposed a somewhat new aim: it was to bend nature to our will for the benefit of mankind.[34] Our culture has gone a long way down their road and few of us will give up the benefits that have accrued. But, we may ask, must the theoretical attitude be lost, must it give way to control, in order to make these gains? N.B. Have we not lost something precious in subordinating *theôria* to *praxis*?

I have called *theôria* an attitude, and so it is: a disposition on our part to receive what things have to tell us. The Greeks listened, often in wonder, to what the ordered whole, the cosmos, could tell them. My theme joins the emphatic sense with that of the weight of the collective sense. It is about the import of individual things and what they might tell us about themselves and about us, for in some sense we are things too. So far, then, we have passed from actionable and serviceable things to beings, to the absolute horizon of the things that are. That transition will lead me to select for further consideration one of the four basic modes of Greek discourse, namely, the distinctive ontological mode. It is along the line of this discourse that *theôria is wedded to philosophy as discourse about being*. As this mode develops, things will emerge in a new light.

34 Spinoza is always an exception to such generalization; still, it is not insignificant that he entitled his great work *Ethics*, in the sense of a wisdom to be lived for the sake of a rational human life. Then, too, Leibniz, gave more honour to the past that did Bacon and Descartes, and sought to restore something of the older conception of philosophy, although on the grounds set forth by Descartes.

2

The Things of Yesteryear

> The poetry of earth is never dead.
> Keats

> While with an eye made quiet by the power
> of harmony, and the deep power of joy,
> We see into the life of things.
> Wordsworth

THE ANCIENTS knew the sad transiency of things. The tragedies placed before the ordinary Greek, with almost unbearable precision, the searing pain of an implacable fate, of vengeful furies and unwavering destiny. Greek society and culture was, indeed, a paean of light,[1] but that light shed its brilliant rays and acquired a piquant intensity against the dark background of a cosmic necessity. That necessity is at work in the epics of Homer and the poems of Hesiod, and we still read the great Greek tragedies of Aeschylus and Sophocles with sorrowful wonder. We acknowledge and respond to the deeply human courage with which the heroes face their destiny, held in the grip of unforgiving fate. The very texture of the language reflects the mighty measured passions that the tragedies both enact and evoke. For beneath the transgressions of a defiant Prometheus, a luckless Orestes, or a mutilated Oedipus, there murmurs the ancient wisdom of the Greeks: *mêden agan,* nothing to excess. Despite the Dionysian revels introduced by the Oriental cults, it is still possible to observe that, in regard to their language,"the passions of the epics were fitted to the mighty but finite [or more exactly, the limited] hexameter. They were like the waves of ocean, which never lose their measure of rise and fall, never lose their metre, be it of calm or storm.

1 Edith Hamilton, *The Greek Way* (New York: Norton 1942), remarks that, even when dying, the Greek called for more light.

Achilles' anger and the torrent of his grief and wrath, rising, falling, and again rising, resistless but not unrestrained, ever roll within the harmonies of the metre".[2] For this is the civilization of admirable form which receives its highest intellectual expression in Plato's theory of forms (*eidoi*). And it is also the civilization of necessity (*anangkê, moira, fatum*), for things must give way to others lest they stay too long and offend the just order in all things.[3] The Latin poet Virgil continues this sad mood, when he speaks of the *lacrimae rerum*, the tears that lie buried within the depths of things, tears that touch the human heart.[4]

But of one thing the ancients were sure: that of the unfailing cosmos. Cicero summed up this unshakeable conviction with these words: "In fact, there is nothing else beside the world [*mundum*][5] that has nothing wanting [*cui nihil absit*], but is fully equipped and complete and perfect [*aptum atque perfectum expletumque*] in all its details and parts."[6] Even the gods dwelt within the parameters of the world.

Many centuries afterwards, Hegel was to distinguish between the concept of *limit* (*die Grenze*), which was favoured by the ancients, and that of

2 Henry Osborn Taylor, *The Classical Heritage of the Middle Ages* (1901; repr. New York: Harper 1958), 238.

3 Anaximander, *Fragment* 1: "The Non-Limited (*to apeiron*) is the original material (*archên*) of existing things; further, the source from which existing things derive their existence (*ex ôn de 'ê genesis*) is also that to which they return at their destruction (*kai tên phthoran*), according to necessity (*kata to chreôn*); for they give justice and make reparation to one another for their injustice, according to the arrangement of Time (*kata tên tou chronou taxin*)." (Kathleen Freeman, *Ancilla to the Pre-Socratic Philosophers* [Oxford: Blackwell 1962], 19.) The German translation is less florid: "Anfang und Ursprung der seienden Dinge ist das Apeiron ..." (H. Diels, *Die Fragmente der Vorsokratiker*, 6th ed., edited by W. Kranz [Berlin: Weidmann 1951], 2:89.)

4 *Aeneid* I, 461. Reflecting upon the destruction of Troy, Aeneas weeping (*lacrimans*) cries: "*quis iam locus, Achate, quae regio in terris nostri non plena laboris? en Priamus! sunt hic etiam sua praemia laudi, sunt lacrimae rerum et mentem mortalia tangunt.*" Fairclough's rather loose translation reads: "He stopped and weeping cried: 'What land, Achates, what tract on earth is now not full of our sorrow? Lo, Priam! Here, too, virtue has its due rewards; here, too, there are tears for misfortune and mortal sorrows touch the heart." (*Virgil: Ecloques. Georgics. Aeneid* 1–6, [Loeb Classical Library no. 63], rev. ed., Harvard University Press 1986, 273.) It is remarkable how many times some version of the word *lacrima* recurs in Virgil's epic.

5 Cicero identifies the term with the Greek *kosmos.*

6 *De natura deorum* II, xiii, 37; Loeb XIX. 158. Cf. Anaximander, *Fragments* 2 and 3: "This (essential nature, whatever it is, of the Non-Limited) is everlasting and ageless (*aidion einai kai agêrô*)," and "(the Non-Limited) is immortal and indestructible (*athanaton ... kai anôlethron*)." (Freeman, *Ancilla to the Pre-Socratic Philosopher,* 19; Diels, *Fragmente,* 1:89.) There is no doubt that, in the ancient sense of the term, that is, in the diffuse sense of whatever is most excellent, the cosmos was divine. Indeed, by virtue of its immortality and incorruptibility, Aristotle concluded that the physicists following Anaximander held *to apeiron* to be divine *(to theion)*. (*Physics* III, 4, 203b13; Diels, *Fragmente,* 3.)

finitude (*das Endliche*), which presupposed the intellectual shift brought about by the absolute and affirmative infinitude attributed by the Christian to the divine.[7] In ordinary English we may often conflate the two terms, but, if we speak more exactly, we may discern the limits of things without attributing finitude to them. For we recognize things as finite only from the point of view of the infinite, and this from a positive view of the infinite which has been acquired incipiently and implicitly through biblical revelation. For the Greeks, on the other hand, the term infinite carried the notion of the formless and not that of the measure of all things.

With the advent of Christianity, rooted in and drawing upon the Jewish revelation, the unshakeable world of the ancients was shaken and yet at the same time it was enhanced, for the creation came to understand itself through the human intelligence as the personal handiwork of the biblical God, a being wholly other from the universe yet intimately engaged within it.[8] Primordiality and ultimacy thereby passed from the cosmos to the lord of the universe, and took on a new meaning. As a result, the things of the world were pulled both ways. On the one hand, an abyss of nothingness opened up before them, for they were created *ex nihilo*, out of nothing – not out of chaos, or out of a primordial sea, or from a mythical monster, or out of any other pre-existent material; nor were they ensconced within an eternally unbegotten world. Cicero's once unshakeable world was seen to have come to be out of nothing antecedent to it except the creator God.

7 It is a question of the nature of the determinate. Hegel remarks perceptively on the transition from determinateness as a qualitative limit (the Greek sense of form) to the finite as the recognition of the non-being inherent in the limited (the Christian acknowledgement of the positive infinite). "Finite things *are*, but their relation to themselves is that they are *negatively* self-related and in this very self-relation send themselves away beyond themselves, beyond their being [that is after several false starts or bad infinites, into the positive conception of the true infinite]." (*Science of Logic*, vol. 1, Bk.I, Sec.1, c.2 B; trans. A. V. Miller [New York: Humanities Press 1969], 129ff.) Nonetheless, it took a number of centuries in the Christian era before the ancient sense of the infinite as indeterminate was explicitly overcome.

8 The division of immanence and transcendence into two separate worlds (into this world and the after-life or other world) is largely a construction of the eighteenth-century Enlightenment. For St Thomas Aquinas and medieval thought generally, the distinction of divine immanence and transcendence was based upon the way *we* view God's relation to the world (That is, they are conceptually not really distinct); in reality, it is the same relation of the world to God. God is most intimately present to his creatures without displacing – or if I may so put it, "jostling" – them, just because he is absolutely transcendent. For my own discussion of the terms, see "La transcendance coïncidente: fondement de l'interrogation," in T. de Koninck and L. Morin, ed., *Urgence de la Philosophie* (Québec: Les Presses de l'Université Laval 1986), 591–8.

And so the very notion of *nothing* took on new meaning; an unprecedented sense of radical contingency came into being.[9] In the ancient world, the notion of Hades had served to express the capacity of things to disappear – but not quite, for they became shades giving way to the living. Even in the Hebrew scriptures, the notion of *Sheol* is a shadowy notion, not quite conceding the total nothingness at the centre of things. According to this new vision, on the other hand, things are nothing taken in themselves and in isolation from their source.[10] But *nothing* is not the last word; for, caught up in the creative act of the biblical God, things are transfigured and destined even unto glory. It is significant that the Hebrew *kabod* (the *glory* of God) also carries with it the sense of *weight*, that is, of the "weightiness" or importance of created things insofar as they reflect the glory of their Maker. We find here a reference to both the *emphatic* and the *value* sense of things noted by the OED. The dramatic state of things is expressed by St Paul, who tells us that the things of this world groan under the labour of a sinful disorder while awaiting their redemption in the revelation of the sons and daughters of God. He warns his readers that "the world as we know it is passing away." And St. Peter speaks of a destruction of the world at the end of time.[11]

Here *things* are not, as with the emphatic meaning of the OED, simply suspended between the universe and the attributes of individuals – but suspended between everything and nothing, between glory and oblivion. This suspension awakened a deep emotion which was celebrated by the early Christian poets, both Greek and Latin – poets in our own day

9 There have been at least four attempts to account for the "scandal" of contingency in so-called Western tradition: (1) Aristotle's account in terms of the unintended conflict of causes; (2) the modern account in terms of probability; and (3) the most recent theory of language, which finds meaning in arbitrary associations. The most radical account, however, is precisely (4) *creatio ex nihilo*, by which all things in the world are creatures dependent for their whole being upon the creative influx of God as primordial Source.

10 Indeed, by a set of transmutations, this recognition of the nothingness of things, once they are torn from their transcendent source, finds an echo in such twentieth-century movements as the theatre of the absurd, existentialism, and some expressions of postmodern thought in which the "nothingness" of life is transmuted into "meaninglessness" and the "unbearable lightness of being".

11 Romans 8:19–22: "For the [whole] of creation is anxiously waiting for God's revelation of his sons ... For we know that all creation groans together and is in labour together until now ..."; also 1 Cor.7: 29–31; and 2 Peter 3:10. There are references in the New Testament to a new heaven and a new earth at the end of time, such as Revelation 21:1–5. This expectation finds its origins in the Hebrew Scriptures: Isaiah 65:17: "For now I create a new heavens and a new earth." As well, there are the Advent texts taken over by the Christian Church in the context of the Gospels and applied to Christ. Cf. Isaiah 9:11–12; 40:3–5: "Let every valley be filled in, every mountain laid low, let every cliff become a plain, and the ridges a valley; then the glory of Yahweh shall be revealed."

almost universally unread. The highest expression of human values among the ancient Greeks, with their love of form, was the ideal of moderation: "nothing too much" (*mêden agan*); and no doubt this contributed to the excellence of the architecture and sculpture which we admire so much today. But this unerring sense of limit gave way before a newly inspired Christian emotion which affected the tonality of language itself. The change is evident in the hymns of the early Christian centuries, the significance of which, as Henry Osborne Taylor points out, "reaches far beyond their utterance; they suggest, they echo, and they listen; around them rolls the voice of God, the infinitude of His love and wrath, heaven's chorus and hell's agonies; *dies irae, dies illa*."[12] Moreover, a recent study of early Christian rhetoric draws attention to the aura that surrounds distinctively Christian expressions – with much use of metaphor, symbolism, and stress as the sign elements in language while confessing the inadequacy of the same signs to exhaust the mystery.[13] The biblical revelation and the incarnation of the very son of God brought upheaval into a disordered, sometimes weary, world. At first gradually, then increasingly, and finally over more than a thousand years, this creative disturbance was brought to a certain completion in the High Middle Ages. The impact of this disclosure was felt across the spectrum of the modes of expression and life, in architecture, painting and sculpture, and in the literary arts, where, to quote Taylor again, "it displays itself in the abandonment of classical metres and the devising of freer forms of verse," so that the whole structure and dynamics of speech and action were transformed. We are familiar, too, with the new forms of organization that gradually evolved: monasticism, a new political order, the universities, the social-welfare institutions, and distinctive ways of life. In short, things are no longer *pragmata or chrêmata,* or even merely *onta*; they are *creaturae*, creatures under the "Great Economy" of God.[14] Whereas the ancient pagan gods were not creators, these "new things" owed their very being to the biblical Lord, their creator.

This poses a problem, even – or perhaps, especially – for us. For there arise two basic attitudes toward the world about us and the things that

12 Taylor, *The Classical Heritage of the Middle Ages*, 246.

13 Averil Cameron, *Christianity and the Rhetoric of Empire: The Development of Christian Discourse* (Berkeley: University of California Press 1991), chapter 2, "Showing and Telling."

14 I have taken the term from Wendell Berry, who relates it to the "Kingdom of God." His "Great Economy of God" can stand in a refreshing way for the traditional sense of Divine Providence. See his *Home Economics* (San Francisco: North Point Press 1987), 54–75. The term "economy" is here understood, not as restricted to the use of money, but in the classical sense of household management, and precisely as the "management of the great household of being."

inhabit it. We can take the world either as *given* or as *gift*.[15] In the first instance, we can take Cicero's stand, that the one unbegotten reality is the world as a whole. If there are gods they are among its inhabitants. This takes the universe as the absolute context.[16] There have been reputable representatives of the self-sufficiency of the universe. Recently, Stephen Hawking implies it, in his *Brief History of Time*. Towards the end of this short book – although he completely misses the proper understanding of the proofs for the existence of God, which he mistakenly thinks hang upon a *temporal* beginning of the universe – this gifted physicist gratuitously opines that there is no need of anything more than what is given to us: "So long as the universe had a beginning, we could suppose it had a creator. But if the universe is really completely self-contained, having no boundary or edge, it would have neither beginning nor end: it would simply be. What place, then, for a creator?"[17]

No doubt, the universe is interesting enough to spend a lifetime and more exploring its structure and striving for a TOE, a theory that will explain everything, even without reference to God. We have already seen that the notion that the universe is self-grounded is not a new idea.[18] But this view receives new sharpness, and loses its innocence, once it is asserted over against the notion that the universe is indeed begotten, being created by God. I say "created" and not merely, as the myths of origin have it, made out of some pre-existent formless substrate; and this

15 As well as English, French marks the difference with the terms *la donnée* and *le don*, German with *das Gegebene* and *das Geschenk*, and Latin with *datum* and *donum*. As will be noted further on, it is curious that the usage of *the given* precisely forestalls a recognition of a *giver*, whereas *gift* invites one to "go beyond" it to a *giver*. For a further elaboration of the point, see my *The Gift: Creation* (Milwaukee, Wis.: Marquette University Press 1982).

16 The Christian understanding of the world's relation to God is quite different. Robert Sokolowski draws attention to what he calls "the Christian distinction": there is no more being when we consider the creation and God than when we consider God alone, since God is the fullness of being. See *The God of Faith and Reason* (South Bend, Ind.: Notre Dame University Press 1982). That is why God is able to be most intimately present in and to the world, without displacing any creature. That is, by virtue of his very transcendence, He does not dwell in it as creatures do, and so He can be present in it in an intimate non-creaturely and non-invasive way. See de Koninck and Morin, ed., *Urgence de la Philosophie.*

17 *A Brief History of Time: From the Big Bang to Black Holes*, (Toronto: Bantam 1988), 141. It is interesting that St Thomas Aquinas, writing in the thirteenth century, anticipates such a view. Before he proceeds with the proofs for the existence of God, he places before the reader two pertintent objections to the proposal that God exists. The first is Stephen Hawking's: since we have the sciences, which explain the world about us, what need have we for anything more? The second counter-position is the scandal of evil: if the world is the creature of a good God, how can there be so much evil in His world? If the first objection calls one's mind to task, the second calls the whole human person to a rigorous assessment. *Summa theologiae*, I, 2, 3, obj. 1 and 2.

18 See n.6 above.

"creation" is the act of a personal God who makes something out of nothing (*ex nihilo*), that is, out of nothing ontologically prior to or simultaneous with God himself. St Thomas Aquinas underscored the absolute gratuity of God's creative act by arguing that even formless prime matter, and *a fortiori* all formed matter, is itself created by God.[19] In a word, the universe is a gift, not merely a given. This is no merely idle quibble, for if the universe is the gift of the person of God, it follows that it is not indifferent to persons and their values. Moreover, the very character and status of things will reflect their giftedness in their radical contingency and the received generosity inherent in them.

Before I take up the second attitude, which takes the universe to be a gift, it will help to touch upon the history of the re-emergence in modern times of the notion of the universe as given. What is interesting about this notion is that, despite its use of the word "given", it precludes, indeed, positively excludes, any reference to a giver. The exclusion is performed by an act of thought that the Schoolmen termed *praecisio*, that is, the cutting away of the thrust of thought towards the question of origins.[20] The vocabulary of the "given" has as its primary reference the human mind. What is given (*data*) is "given" ("present" but not "presented") to a human observer. The language, first associated principally with geometrical construction, seemed to recover strength in the late medieval schools, where it was closely allied to the expanding power of mathematics as an instrument for measuring the configurations of the physical world and its motions. In this sense it is understood to be a postulate: "Let it be granted [given] that ... " From such a postulate, then, many conclusions can be drawn in the sciences with the help of empirical observation. The strategy looks forward towards results, not backwards and upwards towards origins.[21]

N.B.

19 *Summa theologiae* I, 44, 1. Thomas underscored the disconnection between creation and a temporal beginning by insisting that, even if the world were eternal, in the sense that it has no temporal beginning, it would still be a created world insofar as it depends for its very being on the constant gift-giving of God.

20 In the *via moderna* this deliberate exclusion led eventually to favouring a chosen method for expressing the configurations of motion (the laws of motion) in precise mathematical terms.

21 Cf. the use of "let it be posited" (German: *setzen, gesetzt dass* ...). As early as the fourteenth century, it was common to posit counter-factuals, and, by the seventeenth century, possibility had triumphed over actuality. See Étienne Gilson's discussion of "essentialism" in *Being and Some Philosophers* (Toronto: Pontifical Institute of Mediaeval Studies 1949). In the twentieth century we find philosophers discussing a multiplicity of "possible worlds." In these manoeuvres the tie between what is actually given and the logic of "let it be posited" unmasks the priority of imagined possibility over given actuality.

But to make a postulate requires a postulant, and we will have to examine the status of the postulator in the next chapter. For now, I remark simply upon the paradoxical character of a given which excludes a giver. The world suffices to account for itself; or rather, it is taken to need no account as to its origin, but only as to its unfolding in the presence of a human observer. Once again, Stephen Hawking puts the issue succinctly: "A complete, consistent, unified theory is only the first step: our goal is a complete *understanding* of the events around us; and of our own existence ... a complete unified theory [TOE] that would cover everything in the universe."[22] From this it will follow that motion need not seek out a transcendent source in the form of an Unmoved Mover, but rather postulate itself as self-sufficient (*causa sui*). The mind turns, then, towards the empirical discovery of the patterns of motion, and science comes to be understood as the analysis into particles and processes and the formulation of their motion in terms of general laws.

If we turn to the second attitude, that of a created universe and created things, created out of nothing (*ex nihilo*), we find a quite different set of consequences, a quite different atmosphere, attitude and mood, and a quite distinct logic. For creation points towards a giver, and the universe is taken to be a *gift* without pre-conditions imposed upon the giver.[23] No doubt, the origin of this notion of creation is closely tied to the absolute lordship of the biblical God which is to be found in the Hebrew Scriptures; but in them the doctrine itself remained more or less as an implication of that lordship. With the Christians, however, it was seized upon very early for reasons that are not immediately obvious. Was it the dramatic shock of the "new man," the "new Adam," disclosed in Christ? so that attention was drawn to the radical transformation in grace that drew the whole universe towards a new revelation of the Father in and through the Incarnation and the Cross? At any rate, there can be no doubt about the radical change in attitude that soon began to show itself.

Before I proceed further, however, I must make a deliberate aside, in order to avoid misunderstanding. For it is necessary to detach the traditional doctrine of *creatio ex nihilo* from any association with what has

22 Hawking, *A Brief History of Time*, 169, 153.

23 I have traced the distinction between the given and the gift in more depth in the Aquinas Lecture *The Gift: Creation* (Milwaukee, Wis.: Marquette University Press 1982), esp. 34–43.

been called in our day *creationism.*[24] There are several striking differences. Modern creationism has arisen out of a more or less literal reading of the Bible, taking the account in Genesis 1 and 2 to be a description of the *making* of the universe. This reading of Genesis is either understood to be in opposition to the present scientific understanding of the formation of the universe or it requires that selected facts in the scientific understanding be matched with the account in Genesis. The particular target for criticism is the theory of evolution, which is thought to offer an alternative and conflicting explanation.[25] The presumed conflict between religion and science, however, takes us back before the controversy with evolution, and is perhaps best understood through recalling the early-nineteenth-century conflict between the *uniformitarians* and the *anti-uniformitarians.*

I can offer only the merest outline of the conflict. Towards the end of the eighteenth century a suspicion was growing that the earth was older than Archbishop James Usher's chronology, which put its beginning at 4004 BCE.[26] The controversy was fuelled by discoveries in what we today would call paleontology, along with the (fallacious) supposition that the doctrine of creation was conceptually tied to a determinate temporal beginning of the universe. The controversy came to a head at the beginning of the nineteenth century with the new earth science, which we today call geology. Charles Lyell formulated the issue from the side of the new science.[27] He argued that a scientific investigation into the formation of the earth – its land masses, oceans, rivers, lakes, mountains, and valleys – could not proceed without the acceptance of a primary supposition: that the processes of these great earth-formations must have proceeded at a rate of change that is uniform with that of change today.

24 The position is often identified in the popular mind with evangelical Christianity, but it should be noted that this latter movement is not a monolith and that a number of distingished evangelical theologians do not endorse the more extreme views associated with biblical fundamentalism on this issue.

25 One need not fail to see the imperfections in the current theory of evolution, or fail to appreciate the serious objections currently made to it on scientific grounds, to realize that the putative controversy between science and some versions of fundamentalism hinges upon the literal reading of Genesis and a failure to distinguish between the different aims of science and those of the biblical account.

26 Usher or Ussher (1580/81–1656). His chronology, established in *Annales Veteris et Novi Testamenti* (1654, –56; –59), was printed in the margins of many editions of the Authorized Version of the English Bible.

27 *The Principles of Geology*, preface.

Lyell argued that, if we do not make this assumption of the uniformity of the rate of change, we can have no hope of giving a credible, rational explanation of the processes that have formed the earth. His reasoning led him to the following conclusion: present changes in the features of the earth usually proceed at an indiscernibly slow rate, so that the processes that formed mountains and rivers must have needed aeons of past time in order to arrive at the shape in which we encounter the landscape today. Consequently, the earth must be much older than the few thousands of years attributed to it by Usher. In addition, the earth, not to speak of the universe, must have taken much longer to form than Usher maintained. Lyell's appeal was to the reasonableness of the uniformitarian position over against the literal reading of Genesis and the catastrophic measure of time and change.

My present interest, however, is not so much to discredit creationism as to differentiate it clearly from the traditional doctrine of *creatio ex nihilo* which is compatible with the general notion of evolution. For the doctrine of *creatio ex nihilo* arose out of a quite different concern. It is concerned, not with the temporal duration of the earth, but with its absolute dependence upon the Creator for its very existence. The medieval biblical exegetes had less detailed knowledge of the historical context of the Scriptures than our specialists have today, and far less appreciation of the Scriptures' historical development. Nevertheless, they had a rather sophisticated understanding of the various levels of meaning in the sacred text and were open to a variety of interpretations of its parts. For St Thomas Aquinas, the literal meaning of the text was whatever the *littera*, the passage or words, were meant to convey by God in using them; and that could be a historical meaning or a moral one, a spiritual one or a symbolic one. For, if medieval exegetes lacked a sense of history, they did not lack a sense of eternity, and they read the Scriptures as a whole, and as far as humanly possible, from that point of view. To forestall any suggestion that there was a time "before" the world was created, St Augustine had put the matter well enough: time, he argued, begins with creation, since time itself, in an extended sense, is a creature.[28] So that before there were creatures there was no time, no time "before" creation, for time itself issues from God's eternity. Even more

28 Cf. *Confessions* XI, 13: "If before heaven and earth were made there was no time, then what is meant by the question: 'What were You [God] doing *then*?' If there was not any time, there was not any 'then.'" Also, *ibid.*, XII, 13: It is for God "not to know now one thing, now another but, as has been said, to know in one act without any succession of time."

to the point, remniscent of the *Letter of Peter*, St Augustine explicitly divorced the story of creation in Genesis from the schedule of twenty-four-hour days and seven-day weeks.[29]

If I am not mistaken, the second difference between creation *ex nihilo* and creationism is that modern creationism seeks to describe in literal detail the stages by which God *made* the world. For creationism seems to proceed from the conviction that a relatively detailed account of *how* God made the universe is closely connected to a secure account of the fact that he made it. And so it is thought that Genesis, understood in this way, is meant to show us *how* God managed the creation of the world. In the early centuries, the Church Fathers were more modest and content to draw a certain veil of mystery around any attempt to show *how* God created the world.[30] Here again, one does not need to be a secular exegete to discourage such speculation. The philosopher Peter Geach has clearly formulated the difference between *making* and *creating*.[31]

Many centuries before him, however, the Church Fathers were unanimous in insisting that creation is not a labour, neither a process nor a construction, but rather an instantaneous act by which God calls forth finite beings out of nothing. Among others, St Basil of Caesarea (fourth century) underscores the power and ease of the divine act, saying that creation was done in an instant.[32] In his *Discourse with the Arians*, St Athanasius (fourth century) remarks[33] that "God is not wearied by commanding ... but he willed only; and all things subsisted." Similarily,

29 2 Peter 3:8: "But there is one thing, my friends, that you must never forget: that with the Lord, 'a day' can mean a thousand years and a thousand years is like a day." Psalm 90: "To you [Lord], a thousand years are a single day, a yesterday now over, an hour of the night."

30 More precisely, there was no "how," since creation does not use the categories of instrumentality and development. Even the *De Luce* of Robert Grosseteste in the thirteenth century (Eng. trans. Clare Riedl [Milwaukee, Wis.: Marquette University Press 1942]), which describes creation in terms of the dissemination of light, is not quite the same as the modern attempt to match scientific facts with biblical stages. See also A. Crombie, *Robert Grosseteste and the Origins of Experimental Science* (Oxford, U.K.: Clarendon 1953).

31 "Causality and Creation," in *God and Soul* (London; Routledge and Kegan Paul: 1969), 75–85; cited in N. Kretzmann, A. Kenny, and J. Pinborg, ed., *The Cambridge History of Later Mediaeval Philosophy* (Cambridge, U.K.: Cambridge University Press 1982), 825.

32 *In Hexaemeron*, Homily 1, no.6 (*Patrologia Graeca*, vol. 29, col.16). Eng. trans.: *Exegetic Homilies* (Washington: Catholic University of America Press), 11, in *The Fathers of the Church* series.

33 Discourse II; c. 17; *Four Discourses against the Arians*, in *A Select Library of Nicene and Post-Nicene Fathers of the Christian Church*, 2nd series, vol. 4 (Edinburgh: T and T Clark 1987), 361.

Hyppolitus (early third century) had already insisted that "the divine will in moving all things is itself without motion."[34] The instances can be multiplied beyond endurance.

It is a strange and unique act: to create. For it issues from eternity, and from God alone. It is a dimension of duration that not only transcends ordinary human capacity but is particularly alien to our time-conscious culture today. In its proper and original sense, creation (*kitzô*) shares no identity with human or creaturely activity. So that a mystery surrounds the act, just as the Hebrew Scriptures, without explicitly expressing the doctrine of creation out of nothing, nonetheless reserve a special word *(bârâ)* to mark the action proper to God alone. The medieval philosophers based the doctrine of creation upon a feature in things that required a creator: namely, the utterly radical contingency inherent in the finitude of things.[35] Indeed, the Polish art historian Tatarkewicz records that the first known instance of applying the term "creation" to human activity does not occur until the sixteenth century of our era; so strong was the taboo.[36] Once having established the necessity that God exists, the earlier writers frankly conceded an element of mystery surrounding what, after all, is God's work, not man's.[37]

Now, at long last, the clarification of the difference between creationism and creation permits us to return to a consideration of *theôria,* for it, too, underwent a change in the Christian era. It retained what it had been for the ancient Greeks: *openness to the things that are.* But the status of things had changed in the Christian's understanding of them, for things were now poised between the abyss and the glory. How could they not be glorious, being gifts of God? Yet the stakes of good and evil were heightened as well: between redemption and perdition; so that things could also betray the human creature with incalculable results. The entire pathos of the universe was changed. It was this dramatic possibility that led to a new sense of courage (martyrdom), of virtue (the

34 *Against Noetus* c.10 (*Patrologia Graeca,* vol. 10, col.818).

35 See, for example, St Thomas Aquinas's "third way," in *Summa theologiae* I, 2, 3. In keeping with the present emphasis upon experience, Jacques Maritain (*Approaches to God,* 1953; Eng. trans., 1st ed. [New York: Harper 1954] has developed the sense of contingency with regard to each person's existence in a "sixth way" of proving the existence of God.

36 *History of Art,* 3 vols.

37 The sense of mystery, however, did not surrender all possibility of understanding. On the contrary, it pointed to a "light" that is inexhaustively enlightening. St Paul tells us that faith consists in seeing as reflected in a mirror, or as the older translations have it: "in a mirror darkly." (1 Cor. 13:12.) Yet he also tells us that the visible things of this world show forth the invisible realities of God. (Rom. 1:20.)

saints), and of narrative (hagiography). We must admit, too, that the pathos also suffered excesses (amounting at times to a fearful hatred of things, at others to a reckless freedom).

The question one needs to ask at this point is whether this mystery sheds light upon things or simply covers the darkness of our understanding, whether it is a mystery of light or mere obscurantism.[38] And just as the postulate of the given has proved fruitful in the development of empirio-mathematical science, we must ask whether the doctrine of creation *ex nihilo* heightens the meaningfulness (the intelligibility) of things and deepens in them a sense of wonder. Aristotle tells us that philosophical enquiry begins in wonder, but it seems to me that, for him, the wonder does not survive his explanation in terms of the causes.[39]

For the medieval enquirer ("faith seeking understanding"), the wonder increases as the mind moves to contemplate the hidden presence of the source of all things. And so medieval *theôria* returns even more explicitly to its ancient religious origins than Aristotle's *thaumatzein.* The seal set upon the medieval understanding of things receives a kind of canonical expression in the thought of St Thomas Aquinas.[40] This return to religious origins gave rise to the rich tapestry of differing traditions and debate that contributed to the strenuous academic and popular discussions of the time. These public debates respectively bore the names "Quodlibetals" ("Whatever you want to discuss") and the more focused "Disputed Questions." But Thomas had a particular sense of the reality of things, due in part to his early education with the Benedictines, who had combined study and prayer with work (*Ora et labora*), thus joining contemplation and *theôria* with action. In contrast to the pagan intellectuals, who mostly shunned physical labour, these monks have been aptly described as intellectuals with dirt under their fingernails. Later, as a university professor, Thomas was caught up in the recovery of the realism of Aristotle, whom he sought to adapt within a Christian context. In

38 In the hymn with which the Letter to the Ephesians begins, the *mysterion* is no longer understood to be the pagan rites of initiation (for example, the Eleusinian mysteries) but now comes to mean the eternal plan in God's own keeping, the Great Economy.

39 It must be conceded, however, that for Aristotle the wonder does break out once again in those ecstatic moments in which the philosopher fitfully and rarely contemplates the gods. *Theôria,* understood as Christian mystery, on the other hand, is open in faith not just to philosophers but to the simple as well as the learned, and not just in exalted moments of adoration but in the familiar contemplation of quite ordinary things.

40 For a contemporary expression of this view, see Josef Pieper, *Living the Truth* (San Francisco: Ignatius Press 1989); German original: *Wahrheit der Dinge* and *Die Wirklichkeit und das Gute* (Munich: Kösel, 1966, 1963).

so doing he reasserted the continuity of European culture with that of the pre-Christian Greeks, while at the same time transforming the latter at its roots.[41]

In his account of the nature of things, Thomas looked above all, but not exclusively, to Aristotle. More than that, however, he transformed the thought of the ancient Greek into one compatible with the Christian vision of the universe as a created gift. Pursuant to our theme, we must ask: What has happened to the thing in this new setting?

The metaphysical structure that was understood to underly the thing in the Middle Ages seems alien to most of us today, and somewhat fantastic, dragging with it the cobwebs of a discredited cosmological theory. To appreciate its character, therefore, we must try to put aside the contempt engendered in modern minds by its detractors. They are a formidable array of critics, ranging over several centuries from the vituperations of the Renaissance poets and rhetoricians, heady with their own discoveries (Petrarch, Valla, and so on), to the vivid, more methodical contempt of Francis Bacon, who condemned the scholastics as web-spinners. With anti-traditional gusto, he remarked that only the lightest (that is, superficial) thoughts from the past came down to us on the river of time. And after reading Plato and Aristotle, he found it necessary to wash his hands of the detritus of forgotten errors (*De sapientia veterum*). Similar criticisms are voiced by Descartes and Hobbes in the seventeenth century. And the confident Encyclopedists of the eighteenth-century Enlightenment simply dismissed the medieval Schoolmen as unworthy of serious consideration. No doubt, religious division accounted for some of the spirited contempt, but even the sober Catholic René Descartes (1596–1650) averred that the only difference between the great medieval authorities, Plato and Aristotle, was that what Plato had held as merely probable Aristotle asserted as certain.[42]

There were, however, more serious reasons for abandoning the old mode of thought (the *via antiqua*). For underlying and confirming the discredit of Aristotelian metaphysics was the rejection of the more dubious features of what had become Aristotelian cosmology: such doctrines as those of the natural place of things, the embrace of the Ptolemaic astronomy, the insistence upon teleology in nature, and some problems of

41 The enterprise was a troublesome adventure, earning for him and his teacher, St Albert, the ire of opponents who complained that the two Dominicans were so busy trying to turn Aristotle into a Christian that they were only succeeding in turning themselves into heretics.

42 "Letter to Abbé Picot," preface to the French translation of the *Principia*: *Oeuvres* (Adam and Tannery), vol. 9, pt. 2, 5–.

particular motions. What is more, in a positive counter-development, there was the astounding success of scientific analysis in its modern sense, especially in the fields of physics and optics and later in the fledgling chemistry. This steady and often brilliant progress was confirmed in the popular mind by its capacity for fuelling the advance of technology with manifest practical benefits, thus meeting the ideal of knowledge as providing for the "commodiousness" of mankind.[43]

This well-known history of the modern career of knowledge posed, and even today still poses, a problem for philosophers. For in all of this change, philosophy did not quite remain what it was. We know full well how it gradually lost its various branches to the positive and experimental sciences, much as a brood hen loses her chicks: first physics and optics broke away from natural philosophy, followed by the new astronomy and then chemistry. Much later, psychology and sociology and many other subordinate branches broke away from the ancient tree of knowledge, until – to change the metaphor – philosophy stood stripped of its previous garments. What was the philosopher to do? The most obvious option was to fall back from the once vaunted leader's role to that of a camp follower, waiting for the latest finding of science in order to adjust the philosophical system, or, more radically still, to leave the content of our knowledge entirely to the positive sciences: we find in the latter option the anticipation of twentieth-century positivism. Another option was to retreat into a more poetic and intuitive mode of thought: and this is the reaction of nineteenth-century romanticism. Is there not perhaps a third option for philosophy: dare it revisit the early modern shift, and ask whether the polemics of that time warrant us in simply rejecting outright everything present in the older view? In this revisitation, philosophy will keep its primary character as fundamental enquiry.

No doubt, this requires some reconstruction and rediscovery on our part. Fortunately, thanks to the historical turn at the end of the eighteenth century, a well-developed history of philosophy comes to our aid. For philosophy is the sort of enquiry which puts the enquirer, his whole value system, and his relation to past, present, and future, to the test. Philosophy is not simply a collection of conflicting and sometimes fantastic opinions: at best that is doxography. As Hegel has shown us, philosophy is a tradition of enquiry that itself develops in history. And so we might begin the visitation by looking again at the metaphysical structure

43 This emphasis constituted a prominent theme among many seventeenth-century philosophers, notably Bacon, Descartes, and Hobbes. With the advance of technology, "commodiousness" came to mean the provision of commodities and comfort.

of things in their pre-modern version, taking Thomas Aquinas as our guide, without relinquishing our critical faculties to him.

Thomas accepted the Aristotelian analysis of change. But, unlike the modern sciences of motion – Copernican astronomy, Galilean physics, Newtonian optics, and Lavoissier's chemistry – the older analysis of motion did not constitute a sciencc of motion as such. Instead, it translated the phenomena of motion into the language of being; it presented an *ontology* of change, for it understood motion through the categories of being, that is, as *coming-to-be*. The new way (a development of the *via moderna*), on the other hand, assumed motion as fundamental and self-sufficient (*causa sui*); so that instead of seeking out the Source or sources of motion in an ontological sphere that transcended motion, the new sciences traced out the empirical patterns of motion in the very terms of motion and force itself.[44]

Whereas the modern project now sought elements and laws, the older project had sought the ultimate source of motion and the principles operative within it. Aristotle gave his account of motion in terms of the overarching concepts of act (*energeia*) and potency (*dunamis*), in which potency was the possibility of being and the requisite for becoming. Far from ignoring motion, he confessed that it was the most difficult subject matter to explain, because the mind, in forming its ideas, puts a stop to motion by defining its elements and stages. We may put the question: What is it for the house to be *being built*? – not to be already built, for that is the end of the process, its closure. But what is the very process of its coming-to-be, coming-into-reality as a house? It is not when the foundation is laid, or the walls are up, or the roof is on. For those are all definite stages, stoppages, so to speak, partial closures; but they are not the very process of abuilding, not the process itself of being built, of becoming a finished building.

You will have noticed that the aim of the older account is to situate movement within the context and horizon of being, that is, within one of the four primary modes of thinking that originated with the Greeks.

44 Deism was a transitional phase in philosophy, in which God was not so much the source of motion as its initiator. Descartes showed some ambivalence on the issue. In *Le Monde* (c.7, *Oeuvres*, Adam and Tannery, 1909, vol. 9, 44–5), he insisted that God accompanied all motion as a conserving cause; but in a private letter he remarked that, had God initiated the motion of the universe, and then left it entirely alone, it would have developed exactly as it has done according to deterministic laws. It is a small step from this reduced role of God as initiator to the assumption that motion is its own self-generator (*causa sui*). Indeed, in Spinoza's *Ethics*, God or Substance is described as self-causing and is identified with Nature: *Deus sive Natura sive Substantia*.

Unlike the modern empirio-mathematical account, the metaphysical account is not meant to gather data into general patterns or descriptive laws which express quantitative correlations.[45] We can now see that the defect of the ancient and medieval Aristotelians was to conflate sometimes these two distinct projects, using an ontological method for problems which were better answered by the modern empirio-mathematical method. This discrimination is part of the developing history of the modes of explanation in our culture by which the modes discipline and limit each other. Such self-questioning continues to be the issue for philosophy once it is conscious of its own history: to disentangle its own transformed character from that of the burgeoning new sciences of motion as such, and to winnow out the questions and issues that are best addressed to philosophy and those best left to science. Each, then, retains its own integrity.

If there are, strictly speaking, no *things* in modern science, but rather particles and waves in motion, it is still appropriate to philosophy to ask about things.[46] For St Thomas and for most thinkers of the high medieval period (particularly the thirteenth century), the things of nature are complex unities (*res*), descendants of Aristotle's *tode ti* ("this individual of a certain kind," "this horse or tree or man"). Each individual thing is composed of several constitutive principles. Each physical thing is a composite of *form* and *matter*. But we are in troubled waters already, for these terms did not mean to thinkers of the old way what they mean for us today. For most of us, *matter* is a three- or even four-dimensional construction which appears to our senses as something solid but which in fact, we are told, is a cloud of miniscule parts in dynamic interaction with each other.

The metaphysical concept of matter is neither of these, neither apparent density nor real porosity; metaphysical matter is simply the feature of utterly formless formability in things that permits alteration to come about among things, whereby things take on different forms. Such matter provides the continuum by which one state or thing gives way as another state or thing comes into being. Matter is the basis in things by

45 For a consideration of this transition, see John Burbidge, *Being and Will* (Toronto: Paulist Press 1977), esp. chapters 5–7.

46 Heidegger puts the question succinctly in *Die Frage nach dem Ding* (Tübingen: Max Niemeyer 1962), 6: we ask, not what it is to be a thing as a rock, but what it means to be a rock *as a thing*. This 1935–36 lecture was reissued unrevised by Heidegger after the "turn" (*die Kehre*). The subtitle of the printed work, however, shows its Kantian direction: *Zu Kants Lehre von den Transzendentalen Grundsätzen*; the English translation by Barton and Deutsch (Chicago: Regnery 1967) bears the title *What Is a Thing?*

which one thing comes to be out of the passing-away of another, as wood gives way to ashes under the agency of fire. Never existing in a pure state, such matter could nevertheless be understood as the capacity in physical things for receiving new formations in continuity with their past condition, thereby permitting the coming-into-being of new things. Since dimensions belong to and constitute an already formed thing, such a material principle is without dimensions, pure potentiality to the reception of form.

And so we come to the second factor in the constitution of a physical thing; the medievals called this second factor *forma.* Here, too, we find a different meaning and come upon a milestone that carries us back along the way to the earlier understanding of form. With us, I dare to say that form means shape, design, or structure, resulting from the interactions of matter. For the earlier thinkers, on the other hand, form is a distinctive, constitutive factor, that is, it is the intrinsic source of the determinate features of the thing.[47] Modern thought tends to submerge the relative integrity of form in the motion of material particles and waves, considering form as the result of the forces of matter and not as an original constitutive principle.

We see, then, that medieval thinkers distinguished between the material and the physical; for within the physical thing they distinguished between the material or determinable aspects and the formal or determinate aspects. What is more, they looked upon the formal aspects as *immaterial,* but by that term they did not mean the *spiritual* or even the mental.[48] The term "immaterial" is not held in high regard today and is almost absent from our learned speech. Indeed, in current English, if we want to denigrate something, we will say that it is "immaterial," meaning that it is insignificant, that it "makes no matter," makes no difference, is null and void.[49]

Not so with medieval thinkers; they appealed to the immaterial on a number of issues, and nowhere more than in giving an account of the physical constitution of things. Form, for them, was a curious feature of

47 This indicates a quite general difference; modern thought tends to be future-oriented and fruitful in the sense of productive results, whereas ancient and medieval thought tends to be retrospective and source-oriented in terms of situating the enquirer within the community of beings. Contemporary wisdom calls for the attempt to integrate both orientations.

48 See my article "Immateriality Past and Present," in *Immateriality: Proceedings of the American Catholic Philosophical Association,* vol. 3 (1978), 1–15.

49 As such it is not worth considering; recall Russell's witticism, directed, if memory serves me, to Berkeley's philosophy: "No matter, never mind."

clarification of hylomorphism

things, for it was to be found as a constitutive principle within the make-up of physical things and yet was *neither material nor spiritual.* They thought of matter as a restrictive factor, localizing things in a certain space-time context and particularizing them: so that they could say of things, *this* thing here, not *that* thing there. It was, if you like, a general sort of notion, based upon observation. And yet *this* thing (Aristotle's *tode ti,* Thomas's *hoc aliquid*) always designated an individual thing (*tode, hoc*) of a certain kind (*ti, quid*), so that each physical thing could be described by one or another formal category: as this horse, this tree, this rock.[50]

Whereas matter restricts the individual to a space-time location, nevertheless the individual is thought to be constituted also of a formal factor, as that which somehow exceeds that restriction. And whereas the material principle (insofar as it is quantified) restricts things to particular places and times, form is an expansive principle within each thing as it opens its threshold to others and to its ultimate source. In this way, medieval thinkers sustained the Greek sense of cosmic order. I mean that individual horses, while differing in particulars, are of the same general kind, and really manifest that similarity, and deciduous trees are not horses but really different from them and really similar to other leafy things, not merely in certain incidental qualities but in the very pattern of their manner of being. The modern sciences of botany and zoology worry about important traits in the classification of plants and animals, trying to determine the division between the various organisms, and quite rightly so. Medieval natural philosophy, on the other hand, sought out the rough but important constituent principles of things, and attributed the diversity in place to the material principle and the differentiation in features to the formal principles, accounting for the basic differentiation in kind by a primary or essential form, the substantive form of the thing (*forma substantialis*).

What is important for our purpose is to notice that a certain aspect of immateriality is invested within the intrinsic constitution of physical things. This makes for a *real* composite character in physical things which is not, however, a real separation or dualism. Form and matter are co-principles that form the original essential unity of each physical thing. It is the trans-material feature of form that gives rise to the intelligibility of things and the basis of their real interrelations: foxes breed

50 It is in keeping with Heidegger's pre-conception that, having given priority to space and time, he renders the Aristotelian concept of the individual (*tode ti,* "this something of a certain kind") violently as "*dies da,*" "this-here," thus overriding the plain meaning of *ti* in its specific and non-temporal/non-spatial formal sense, which presumably is to be relegated by Heidegger to the merely ontic. (*Die Frage* G37/E49.)

with foxes, and not with chickens; instead they eat them. To acknowledge such specific formality does not commit us to the fixity of species. Today we are more conscious of the development of things than medieval thinkers, but we are no more conscious of their transiency. It may well be that a day will come in which there are no more foxes, but as long as we have an ordered world there will be things of a definite kind[51]; and so the medieval analysis bears consideration. The medieval vision is close to what nature has proposed, and it is in nature that we find things and not in the laboratory (except in an extended sense).

The parent of the Latin *natura* is the Platonic *eidos*, which, following Aristotle, becomes constitutive of the specific character of each thing. So, too, it is in the primary form that medieval thought finds the basis for the notion that each thing has a specific *nature*, from which issues a more or less regular pattern of behaviour: fire burns, birds nest, trees grow. The notion that each thing possesses a specific nature was all but dismissed at the beginning of the modern period with the general dismissal of scholasticized Aristotelian principles and causes. After all, such a notion did not make sense within the new science of motion as such, for the new way of thinking had different aims. Nor has the notion of specific natures been rehabilitated in the mainline of modern and contemporary thought.[52] Even in Hegel and Heidegger there are no natures in the sense given to the term by the metaphysicians of the Middle Ages, nor are there any in the family resemblances of Wittgenstein. Many modern thinkers conceive of the thing as a coalition of properties modelled after the structure of the proposition. What is missing is the recognition of an intrinsic formal specifying principle at the core of each thing, its principal form or nature, the emphatic sense.

If we were to accept that the things of nature have specific constitutions with which even the technologues must work – for to change the natural activity of a thing is to change it from what it first presents itself to the technologue as being – if in this minimal sense we were to accept that things have natures, and that these natures manifest themselves for the most part in regular patterns of activity, so that fire consumes, plants grow, and animals feel, then we might be more liable to accept the notion of a certain restricted sense of teleology in physical things. Teleology or

51 Even experimentation in genetic reconstruction relies upon the given determinate characteristics of the genes.

52 Phenomenology (cf. Husserl's eidetic intuition, *Wesenschau*) provides a descriptive opening for a doctrine of essences but is generally not understood along the lines of a metaphysics of natures.

finality, then, does not mean (as with Bacon) conscious purpose, nor does it mean some cosmic theory of natural places (as with Aristotle), but, more modestly, it means the self-maintenance of a more or less regular unitary pattern of activity. TELEOLOGY

Neither the ancient nor the medieval thinkers had the sense of universality in nature that was falsified by a single exception; for them, universality meant the regularity of behaviour that provided the basis for general observations: that "for the most part" trees grow when they are watered, die when they are not, that animals hunt for food, and similar homely observations. And these things do this, not only for the semi-extraneous end of preserving the species (through reproduction), but for the goal of preserving themselves in a specific way of living and acting. Moreover, even inorganic elements and compounds give witness to the same stability of behaviour in repetible conditions, and we expect them to behave so.

It is this sense of teleology that is evident among medieval thinkers. Thus, St Thomas's fifth way, the so-called teleological proof, is not a proof from cosmic design, the watchmaker proof current in the eighteenth century, for he did not envision the universe as a great machine.[53] The fifth way is rather a proof arising from the modest claim that physical things, for the most part, exhibit a tendency to act in a regular and specific manner. One might say that they have a certain style, and – if you will pardon the anthropomorphic metaphor – are "comfortable" in that pattern. That is, they find it good. This is the basis for attributing a normative good to all things – even to things not good for us – and eschewing the putative modern distinction of valueless fact and factless value.

But if the medieval principles of matter, form, and finality differ from our notion of them, nowhere is the difference greater than in what is known as the principle of *efficient* causality, by which is meant: effective causality. For this is the originary principle that leads back to the source of things. Whereas modern enquiry searches out the particular forces that initiate change within the context of motion, medieval inquiry sought out the *universal source* of all being and coming-into-being. So that, in addition to the causes of Aristotle – matter, form, and finality – the mediaeval sense of effective, originating causality differs both from

53 More significantly, Thomas did not include the argument from design in his "five ways," even though the proof was known in the Middle Ages, having come down to them from ancient sources.

the ancient Greek sense of a generative cause of motion and from the modern sense of an initiatory moving force. Such an effective cause is not simply a generative cause of motion, nor is it merely an initiating impulse; it is a genuine originating and communicating cause of being (*influxus entis, communicatio essendi*). With St Thomas and other medieval thinkers, the effective, originating cause is the cause of the very being of things. For the radical contingency of things needs more than an account of their motion, and calls more deeply for an account of their existence, even for the existence of Cicero's and Hawking's unshakeable universe, for it, too, comes to be in the continual coming-to-be of the things within it.[54] The primordial originating or effective cause of their being, then, must be the Absolute Being, whom Thomas calls the Pure Actuality of Being itself (*Actus purus, Ipsum esse subsistens*).

This means that the medieval understanding of things, all things, including physical things, is such that there is a great, even infinite depth present within them.[55] For the cause of their being could not simply start them off and then abandon them, as a mere initiating cause would do, but must dwell within them, sustain them every moment of their own existence. The immanent presence of their Source within each thing is the correlative of the radical contingency of things understood as creatures. Deep within each physical thing, dwells the glory of the Creator God. In the words of the poet:

> The world is charged with the grandeur of God.
> It will flame out, like shining from shook foil;
> It gathers to a greatness, like the ooze of oil
> Crushed …
> And for all this, nature is never spent; [in each]
> There lives the dearest freshness deep down things … [56]

54 The universe constantly comes to be, however, not by means of motion, but, as earlier noted, by a continuing act that transcends motion. See nn.31–3 above.

55 The nineteenth-century poet Gerard Manley Hopkins put the insight vividly in *Pied Beauty*: "Glory be to God for dappled things–/ For skies of couple-colour as a brinded cow;/ For rose-moles all in stipple upon trout that swim;/ Fresh-firecoal chestnut-falls; finches' wings;/ Landscape potted and pieced – fold, fallow, and plow;/ And all trades, their gear and tackle and trim./ All things counter, original, spare, strange;/ Whatever is fickle, freckled (who knows how?);/ With swift, slow; sweet, sour; adazzle, dim;/ He fathers-forth whose beauty is past change:/ Praise him." See Louis Untermayer, ed., *Modern British Poetry: A critical Anthology*, 5th ed. (New York: Harcourt Brace 1942), 47.

56 Once again, Hopkins, *God's Grandeur.*

It is no accident, then, that several of the Hebrew words which we translate in English, as glory stress the luminous and beautiful; nor is it strange that a Hebrew word for the glory of God (*kâbôd*) also carries with it the sense of *weight*, that is, of weightiness, of importance and authority.[57] We have come upon a deepening of the double sense given to the word by the *OED*: it is both emphatic and import-bearing. For the thing carries with it the weight of the fullness of being. The medieval sense of thing (*res*) leads back to an original Plenitude which at once resides within each thing even as it transcends and overflows that same thing.[58]

This insistence upon the intrinsic depth of things cuts across the separation of transcendence and immanence which became so pronounced in the eighteenth-century Enlightenment. That separation removed the depth in things, making the transcendent and the immanent exclusive spheres and drawing the horizon of enquiry tightly around the finite world. As already mentioned,[59] medieval metaphysicians saw the relation between finite effect and infinite source as a single relation, distinct merely in the way in which the relation is approached. For them, the divine source of things is most immanent within them. It is not only the mystic but the metaphysician, too, who agreed that God in the fullness of his being is more intimately present to a thing than the thing is to itself. But this inner presence to and within created things is possible only because of the utter transcendence of the unbegotten God from the things he creates, the unmakeable things we do not make. So transcendent from things is God that he is not – as were the Greek gods – one more being filling up the universe, but rather not a being at all in that

57 See E. Jenni and C. Westermann, ed., *Theologisches Handwörterbuch zum Alten Testament*, 2 vols. (Munich: Chr. Kaiser 1971), 1:794–812: "*schwer sein.*" I am indebted to Francis Martin for a discussion on this point.

58 Cf. St Augustine's *cor pondus amoris.* Gabriel Marcel has remarked ("The Ontological Mystery," in *The Philosophy of Existence* [New York: Philosophical Library 1949], 3) that, while philosophy has spent much time on the problem of the one and the many, it might better have spent more time on the question of the full and the empty. Once we shift attention from how the many proceed from the one, we meet again the two accounts of origin: either from an original fullness and source (*creatio ex nihilo*) or from a relatively empty starting point (from absolute indeterminacy to developed determinacy). Hegel's *Science of Logic* starts with just such an empty concept, and although the *Logic* is not intended to be an account of actual development, nonetheless its conceptual scheme of absolute self-determination displaces the creation account and interprets things as moments of the process of Spirit's own self-determination.

59 See n.8 above.

sense (*pace* Heidegger!), but the fullness of being, and so able to be present to his creatures without displacing them in any way.[60]

Here again, what I might call the "thick" sense of things joins with an interpretation of the OED's emphatic sense; and here we find the convergence of two traditions: the Greek or Aristotelian sense and the Hebrew or biblical sense, both deepened with the understanding of *creatio ex nihilo.* A medieval development of this double origin is to be found in the scholastic doctrine of the transcendentals.[61] Accordingly, each thing (*res*) is signed with meta-properties that transcend its specific nature, thus embedding each thing in a community of shared being. For in each thing the essence and existence are undivided, so that *each unit is undivided being (unum est ens indivisum)*. But that unity is distinguished from every other being within the community of beings which shares these transcendental properties (*ens aliquid*). These interrelations take the form of three pre-eminent super-relations. Each being is intelligible, that is, truth-bearing (*verum*); each is valuable, offering itself as good within its own context (*bonum*); and each shines with the luminosity of being, signed by beauty (*pulchrum*). Thus, each being shares in the transcendental properties of being: unity, truth, goodness, and beauty.

So put, this may seem pie in the sky to us, whose mood often resembles the century of the Black Plague more than the buoyancy of the High Middle Ages. But those same medieval thinkers were conscious of the tragic possibility of evil that lay within these deep and luminous things.[62] Indeed, it was their attractive goodness that made their misuse more terrible, for the medieval person had a highly developed sense of the dramatic character of the use of things, which could lead to perdi-

60 As already mentioned in n.16 above, Robert Sokolowski develops this relation of the world to God and calls it "the Christian distinction" in *The God of Faith and Reason.* It is already operative in St Anselm's reply to Gaunilon (appendix to the *Proslogion*). Gaunilon had thought Anselm was speaking of the highest being – in Heidggger's terms, within the "ontotheological circle" – but Anselm corrects Gaunilon, saying that he is talking not about the "highest being" but about the absolutely transcendent being, "that being than which none greater can be thought." Nicholas of Cusa expresses a similar thought. God is so transcendent that he is not even Other from the universe in the correlative sense in which Plato in the *Sophist* conceives the categories of Same and Other; he is so transcendent that Nicholas is driven to speak of God as *Non-aliud,* that is, as not-Other.

61 See an influential presentation of these in St Thomas Aquinas, *De veritate* I, 1, in which such facets as truth and goodness (and in other passages, beauty) are resident in each and every thing.

62 The Nobel Prize poet Czeslaw Milosz has gathered a heterogeneity of mostly contemporary poems and entitled the collection *A Book of Luminous Things* (New York: Harcourt Brace/Harvest 1996).

tion as well as to salvation. It was the luminous depth in things that awakened wonder and led to the positive notion of mystery, underlying even physical things. And here, too, *theôria* passes over into mystery, and knowledge into delight.

These, then, are the things of yesteryear, more than mere common sense yet grounded in our ordinary observations of the world about us, and more than simply ordinary, but bearing an infinite weight and bottomless depth. For, although wonder is a disposition in us, it is awakened in us by things. Medieval wonder is aroused not simply by the unknown and exotic (though there is some of that, too) but even more by the known and familiar. If I have spent this time recalling things familiar to you, I have tried to look at them with fresh eyes, to listen to them with open ears, and to ask whether, after all, such things can awaken wonder in us? If they can and do, it is the beginning of *theôria* by which thought seeks its source as it ponders the origin and dignity of things and the paradox of their fate in modern thought and culture.

3

Come, Let Us Talk about the Death of Things

It is not now as it hath been of yore …
The things which I have seen
I now can see no more.
… [But] now I see with eye serene
The very pulse of the machine.
Wordsworth

THE LATE MEDIEVAL PERIOD in Western Europe underwent a crisis of the mind. In the late Middle Ages, theological and philosophical reason, exercised with such confidence by St Thomas Aquinas and others a century or two before in the High Middle Ages, withdrew in large measure from the old ways and the old commitment to metaphysics, done more or less in the style of a Platonized Aristotle (the *via antiqua*). In its place, a modern way of thought (the *via moderna*) struggled to free itself from the grip of what was taken to be an outmoded – indeed, in some ways and, in hindsight, an admittedly over-extended – mode of thought, a mode that had lingered too long in new spheres of enquiry to which it had no right. Even more, a new sense of individuality and particularity pressed towards the light. No doubt, other forces played their role too – such as increased trade (especially with the East); urbanization and its concomitants; a growing sense of individual independence ("city air makes free"); an economy more and more based upon fluid currency (quit-rent); the assertion of sovereign nation-states (particularly France and England); and an increase in lay education. A new way of thinking became the mode, its prevalent expression taking the form of *nominalism.*[1]

1 The actual situation was complex. For a more nuanced yet general study, see F. Copleston, *A History of Philosophy*, bk.1, vol. 3 (New York: Doubleday/Image 1985), 43–152. After carefully qualifying the influence of nominalism upon physics, he writes: "It is true, of course, that certain philosophical positions maintained by Ockham himself or by other

The relevant feature of this widespread intellectual movement is its conception of unity and difference which prepared the way for the dissolution of the medieval understanding of the density and depth of things. Nominalism is interested principally in the logic of sentences and terms, and has been called "terminism." It moves principally within the linguistic or logical mode of discourse.[2] According to nominalism, any item, be it a concept or a word, is distinguished from another by its self-reference, so that every unity is thought to be an incomplex unit, a simple self-identity; and every distinction is in mind and in fact taken to be a separation that excludes all others from the self-identical simplicity of each unit.[3] Gone is the earlier metaphysical mode of thought whose original units are intrinsically and really complex (*tode ti*). It follows, according to the new way, that each unit is thought to be related negatively to all others

followers of the *via moderna* were calculated to influence the conceptions of scientific method and the status of physical theories. The combination of a 'nominalist' or conceptualist view of universals with the thesis that one cannot argue with certainty from the existence of one thing to the existence of another thing would naturally lead to the conclusion that physical theories are empirical hypotheses which can be more or less probable but which cannot be proved with certainty ... It is true, however, that one can see a new view of the world coming to birth in the fourteenth century and that this was facilitated by the adoption of the theory of impetus in the explanation of movement ... One can see in the adoption of the impetus theory a step on the road towards a new conception of the material world. Or it might be better to say that it was a step on the road towards the development of physical science as distinct from metaphysics" (ibid., 163–7). See the magisterial study of Armand Maurer, CSB, *The Philosophy of William Ockham in the Light of Its Principles* (Toronto: Pontifical Institute of Mediaeval Studies 1999), which (unlike most other studies of Ockham which concentrate upon his logic) takes up his underlying metaphysics and its antecedents and implications.

2 N. Lobkowicz, *Theory and Practice* (South Bend, Ind.: University of Notre Dame Press 1967), 111ff., remarks that "Ockham's reductionism together with his emphasis upon the fact that science is not about the things themselves but at most about mental contents standing for things, produced the tendency to put aside the problem of 'literal truth' and instead to look for scientific workableness and logical consistency. Throughout the fourteenth century nominalists liked to use the phrase '*secundum imaginationem*' and to work in natural philosophy in terms of 'imaginable cases' which they were fully aware were physically impossible." In the twentieth century some philosophers continue to pose issues in terms of other possible worlds, even counter-factual ones. This is compatible with the view of the world as simply "there" (given) and points towards a more prominent role for the idealizations of mathematics in the construction of hypotheses and their expression in mathematical formulae; in a word, towards the mathematization of the study of nature.

3 Anton Pegis has clearly delineated the incipient conflict concerning the nature of the basic realities, whether as original complexes (*via antiqua*) or elemental indivisibles (*via moderna*). See "The Dilemma of Being and Unity," in R. E. Brennan, ed., *Essays in Thomism* (New York: Sheed and Ward 1942), 151–83.

by the exclusion of those others.[4] Nevertheless, the new way held its own attractions; for with it there appeared on the horizon an alluring sense of liberation from the intimate interwoven character presented by the old way of thinking, which held that each being is embedded within the community of interrelated beings.

While it was not inevitable, neither is it entirely surprising, then, that the old gave way to the new. Moreover, as the power of the mind to uncover the intrinsic make-up of really complex things was thought to decrease, the power of the will to combine separate ideas and words in seemingly unexpected and contingent ways increased. An intellectual "space" was opened up for a much freer play of the will than thirteenth-century masters had imagined. With that opening, a modern tendency emerges to define freedom as indeterminism. This indeterminacy is nowhere expressed so forcefully as in the triumph of the divine will over the divine mind in much of fourteenth-century theology. The primacy of the will over the relation between the components of things has persevered even until our own day, increasingly centring upon the human will. In the seventeenth century, posing the question in theological terms, John Locke asked whether God could endow mere unstructured matter with the power of thought. This is a possibility that medieval thinkers would have thought absurd, holding as they did that matter needed structural preparation for the reception of the power of human thought. After all, had not Aristotle defined the soul as the form correlative with a body already disposed as potential to the reception of life?[5] In subsequent centuries, as theological issues waned, the new-found power of the will took human form, finding its realization in the growing power of a technology that was fuelled by the new sciences. In sum, *voluntarism* became a fellow-traveller of *nominalism.*[6]

4 Here is the seed of the "power of the negative," associated with Hegelian and Marxist dialectics. In contrary fashion, some postmodern philosophers (for example, Jacques Derrida, who builds upon Saussurean linguistics) deconstruct the putatively closed self-referential unities of modern semantic theory and understand language to be a system of arbitrarily related differential signs, whose meaning is always postponed or deferred to others in the system; hence the famous Derridean "différance."

5 See his *De anima* II, 1 (412a20 and 412a30): "The soul [and in humans the intellectual soul] is the first grade of actuality of a natural body having life potentially in it. The body so described is a body which is organized."

6 Voluntarism was prevalent in the psychological, social, and political spheres, as well as the theological. In "Two Concepts of Liberty" (from *Four Essays on Liberty* [Oxford, U.K.: Oxford University Press 1969], 129n.1) Isaiah Berlin commends the work of Michel Villey, "who traces the embryo of the notion of subjective rights" to William of Ockham, the precursor of nominalism. See also the pervasive use of *conatus* in seventeenth-century philosophers, as noted below in n.33.

These twin developments (of nominalism and voluntarism) might have remained in the lecture halls had they not also contributed to a disposition that revived, at the end of the mediaeval period, the ancient sense of atomism.[7] Atomism, too, might have remained a learned, if somewhat covert, theory (for it was tainted by a suspect association with atheism) had there not been a gradual alteration of attitude that produced remarkable cognitive results and, before long, technical benefits. It is said that during the fifteenth century more technical inventions – modest ones to our mind, such as improvements in pulleys and pumps – were realized than in the thousand years before.[8] No doubt, this encouraged the development of modern mechanics.

Early modern mechanics (not unlike nominalism in the logical sphere) aimed in the physical domain to break down large complexes into independent parts, which, upon being reassembled, re-established the original whole as a synthetic product. The correlative of such analysis is a resultant synthesis, whereas the subject of the older metaphysical reflection is an original composite being. In the older way, the original complex unities maintain their unity throughout the analysis, their constituents not being actually separated out from each other in the process. The reflection proceeds within the original composite. The older mode of analysis does not separate out the constituents into actually (or even potentially) independent parts, as chemistry separates compounds into elements. Thus, in the *via antiqua,* there is no matter in physical things that can exist separately from form, as chemical elements can exist independently of their compounds; nor are there physical accidents without substance, nor existence without essence. In the new way, on the other hand, all composite unities are treated as synthetic results which in principle can be broken down into their separate components as elements or particles in their pure state. This mode of analysis fitted

7 "Revived" with a difference, however. The ancient atomism was a metaphysical theory caught up in the attempt to resolve the ontological problem of change posed by Parmenides's identification of Being with the changeless; whereas the revived implicit atomism of the early modern period was taken up into the newly developing empirio-mathematical sciences. What had been a philosophical theory became under modern conditions a scientific postulate. Moreover, in keeping with the shift of theoretical intelligence from a principled study of being to a descriptive study of motion, the ancient focus on the size and shape of atoms (the latter property being too qualitative for the new aspiration to quantitative precision) gave way to "speed and direction of motion," which "were taken to be basic explanatory features," just because they were amenable to "a genuinely quantitative account." See S. Gaukroger, *Descartes* (Oxford, U.K.: Clarendon 1995), 72.

8 Lobkowicz, *Theory and Practice,* 93–6, details a somewhat more gradual increase in technical innovation, though the general picture is similar.

in with the prevailing theoretical nominalism, and picked up new power as it became the practical logic of modern mechanics and its application in modern technology.[9] It is a mode of analysis that propels the search for fundamental particles and that has fuelled scientific advances almost to our own day.[10]

Of course, it is not that there had been no analysis heretofore; after all, the word itself is Greek. Indeed, the original Greek thrust towards concept-formation is a form of analysis. In the high metaphysics of Aristotle and Plato, developed and transformed by Thomas Aquinas and others, metaphysics rests upon a mode of analysis that resolves thought into first principles. But these principles remain embedded in the thing and are not separated out into independent items. And so the analysis of the *via antiqua* differs from the new mode of analysis. The very possibility of the older metaphysics rests upon the feasibility of discerning *real, extra-mental* distinctions within things themselves, real distinctions and not merely mental categories that are made for the convenience of the mind. Such principles as matter and form, substance and accidents, essence and existence are really distinct but not really separate, and in the *via antiqua* the things to which thought directs its attention are taken to be really unitary composites and not collections of potentially independent particles.[11]

In Thomas Aquinas's thought, the most radical and original distinction is that between *essentia* and *esse*, between the essence and the existence of the thing, that is, between the way a thing is and the fact that it exists at all. For, if I may borrow Leibniz's later formulation, the question "Why anything at all, why not rather nothing?" takes on a radical

9 Beeckman, with whom Descartes "apprenticed," was essentially an artisan. He sought "the explanation of macro-geometrical regularities in terms of a micro-mechanical model, and he was almost certainly the first person in Europe to pursue this approach in detail" (Gaukroger, *Descartes*, 70). Moreover, Beeckman insisted that "microscopic mechanical phenomena be explained in terms of microscopic mechanical processes which are essentially similar to them," unlike Aristotle's principles, which were of a different order from the entities they constituted; that is, they belonged essentially to the activity of the agent in constituting the entities. This development points away from explanations through agent causes and towards explanations in terms of patterned laws.

10 For further contrast between ontological principles and elemental particles, see my essay "Analysis by Principles and Analysis by Elements," in L. Gerson, ed., *Graceful Reason: Essays in Ancient and Mediaeval Philosophy Presented to Joseph Owens*, (Toronto: Pontifical Institute of Mediaeval Studies 1983), 315–30).

11 There is no doubt that contemporary physics and its related sciences have moved somewhat beyond the cruder early modern form of elementalism, since the subatomic particles are understood to exist in concert with each other. Nevertheless, the concept of the unit, particularly in the popular mindset, retains this view and still influences thought in other areas, even as it encourages the dismissal of a realist metaphysics.

meaning in medieval metaphysics. It raises the question to the level of absolute being and non-being. Thomas answers by pointing to the thing's actuality of existing (*actus essendi*) as really distinct (yet not separate) from the way (*essentia*) in which it exercises that existence. The way a thing exists, the kind of thing it is, is no warrant for its status as an existent. There are many imaginary kinds of being that do not exist in the real world. No doubt, this deeper question was inspired by the biblical revelation of *creatio ex nihilo*, but it was also inherent in the logic of ontological enquiry which sought to resolve the question into terms of *being* and *non-being* taken absolutely. And so Thomas found philosophical grounds for a new depth that is inherent in the logic of ontological enquiry: Why *being* at all?[12]

Aristotle's question (*ti*?) had asked after the form and substance of things (*eidos, ousia*), whereas with St Thomas's *utrum?* thought plunged more deeply into the very texture of existence itself, seeking to resolve the question into the root-terms of being and non-being understood as existence and non-existence. Once *being* becomes the ultimate horizon of thought, as it does in the ontological account, it submits itself to enquiry. In fact, this deeper enquiry was inspired by acknowledgement of the absolute Creator and *the status of creatures*; but the deepening of the question was then seen to follow from the logic of ontological enquiry. So that, within the general context and illumination provided by biblical revelation, Thomas found philosophical grounds for pushing the enquiry further than Aristotle, who had assumed the ultimate and original character of the cosmos. Once the question of *being* is followed to its destiny, the sense of contingency takes on a more radical meaning. For change points to the insufficiency of things and ultimately to their origin from that which is all-sufficient. The distinction between *esse* (or *actus essendi*) and *essentia* (or *modus essendi*) arises from the conviction and experience of the radical contingency of things, their inherent nothingness (the *radical nihil* or insufficiency at the root of creaturely existence). In this way, Thomas both preserves and transforms the Aristotelian insight that the original and primary inhabitants of the cosmos are individual composite things (*tode ti, hoc aliquid*); but he now understands these same things more radically and absolutely as beings (*onta, entia*) and in terms of being (*ens in quantum ens, esse simpliciter*).

12 It is significant that August Comte, in elaborating his positivism, counsels his readers to abandon the question *why?* in order the better to pursue the question *how?* And his contemporary, John Stuart Mill, insists that there can be no rational discourse concerning ends, but only concerning the means, i.e. the *how*. This foreshortening of the range of reason had been anticipated by David Hume, who asserted that ideas have no power to alter passions.

What is primordial and original in such a world are not the bare particulars posited by nominalism, nor the elemental units of mechanism, but the complex entities already acknowledged by Aristotle (*ta onta* now realized as *res*, that is, as *realia*).[13] The outstanding feature of the *via antiqua* is that the original unity is not simple but complex and that the original units of the real world contain within themselves basic and essential otherness, as *form* is other from *matter*, *substance* distinct from *accidents*, and *existence* not at all *essence*. These constituents within the thing are considered to be *really* distinct prior to any intervention of the human mind. The primary ontological principles constitute the thing as such, the mediaeval *res*, which is a far cry from Russell's merely logical and shadowy construction. These principles constitute what I might call the "thick" sense of things, the unmakeable things in the sense that they are creatures and not constructs. We have arrived at the metaphysical understanding of what the OED had called the "emphatic" sense of thing.

Such distinctions provide the charter for the older way of thinking and, without the possibility of making these distinctions within the thing, this mode of thought is disinherited, to become an absurd clown in the intellectual world. The young A.J. Ayer denounced such metaphysics as nonsense, that is, as an absurdity lying below the threshold of meaning[14]; and it is the cry of the positivists that such metaphysics is in need of therapy. The *via moderna* also rejected such a claim to intrinsic real distinctions, and sought rather to employ the razor of mental precision, so that whatever could be distinguished in the mind as pertaining to things could in principle be separated out in reality. It was this conviction that had already fuelled the search for the ultimate particles of the physical universe. The science of mechanics proceeded on this basis with considerable, if limited, success in the early modern period, and quite legitimately, since it made no sweeping claims about the ontological character of the elements that it separated out. Once such a mode of analysis came to be translated into philosophy, however, the thrust towards mechanical analysis ceased to be a special science and became the comprehensive philosophy of mechanism, that is, became a statement about the ultimate nature of reality.

13 *Res* and *ens* are in reality the same but differ by the emphasis given to their constituents. *Ens* or being signifies the whole composite, with emphasis on the act of existing (*actus essendi*), whereas *res* or thing signifies the same composite but with emphasis on the *modus essendi* or *essentia*.

14 His early work, *Language, Truth and Logic*, was once described as Oxford's bible during the 1930s. It asserted that any statement not confined to the canons of logic and immediate sensory knowledge was neither true nor false but simply meaningless. This positivism cast, not only metaphysics, but also poetry, theology, and ethics, into absurdity.

As a philosophy, mechanism makes sweeping claims, based upon three presuppositions. First, it supposes that everything in the universe is reducible to absolutely simple parts, call them *particles, minima, corpuscles,* or even *atoms* (*indivisibilia*). This stands in contradiction to the earlier metaphysical insistence upon the *intrinsically* complex character of the original units (*res*). Secondly, it supposes that these parts are absolutely self-related and separate from one another; so that in the physical world they are related to each other solely by external relations of location. The metaphysical analysis, on the other hand, had recognized both external relations of location *between* physical things and also intrinsic relations *within* the constitution of the original composite things (*tode ti, hoc aliquid*). Thirdly, mechanism supposes that in the physical universe these parts displace one another by movement in place. Accordingly, the variety of Aristotelian motions, which included other forms of change, such as change of quality, are reduced to combination and recombination of elements by way of displacement.[15] Non-scientists will recognize the mechanistic profile, no doubt, from high school or college physics and chemistry. And, although its popularization is sometimes crude, the fundamental presuppositions and viewpoint remain the same. As a scientific and partial mode of analysis, it has proven fruitful, but as a philosophy that claims for it an exclusive and comprehensive role in determining the nature of reality, it is, to say the least, open to question.

The root difference between the old and the new way revolves around the different concept of the unit. In the older, ontological way, the primary unit (*tode ti, hoc aliquid* = *res*) is inherently complex though undivided (*unum est ens indivisum*); while in the new way, each ultimate basic unit is not only undivided but allegedly indivisible, at least until science advances and succeeds in dividing it into even more ultimate *indivisibilia.* In the older way, the original unities (*res*), being composite, are undivided though subject to division, since things are liable to loss of qualities (through alteration) and even of substance (through corruption). In the new way, the units are not only undivided but indivisible, since they are in principle utterly incomplex, absolutely simple, supposedly the ultimate

15 In addition to displacement (change of place), recognized by mechanism, the Aristotelian analysis of movement recognizes other distinctive kinds of motion that are not reducible to displacement, namely, alteration of qualities (such as change of color), augmentation or diminution of size (such as growth), and generation and corruption of substances (such as the passing away and coming-to-be of things). All four kinds of change are understood as distinctive kinds of ontological differentiation and are not reduced to the displacement of quantitatively determinate particles.

units of reality. Once again, this has proven to be a powerful motive for scientific research. As I have already indicated, for the past four hundred years, until our own century and even now to some degree, much of basic science has been propelled by the search for ultimate particles, the indivisible atoms that are the "building blocks" or basic units of the scientific understanding of the physical world.[16]

Nor did this spirit of ultimate indivisibility remain a mere physical theory. In Descartes's philosophy, ideas themselves are defined in much the same way. The first rule of his famous and influential *Discourse on Method* (1637) states the criterion for distinguishing the true from the false: "I resolved to accept as true only that which presents itself to my mind so clearly and distinctly that it cannot be doubted." He held that a true idea is clear insofar as nothing in it remains obscure, and that it is distinct insofar as it cannot be confused with any other idea and has no intrinsic interdependent relation with any other idea. Carried to its logical extreme, this becomes the mechanism of the mind: indivisible self-identities in the form of mental particulars are related to one another through their exclusion of other ideas to which they can be linked separately in accordance with Descartes's method.[17]

If in the history of philosophy, that is, of fundamental enquiry, we are to mark off the classical profile of the modern period, the boundaries will be marked by the methodical philosophy of Descartes, on the one hand, and the critical philosophy of Immanuel Kant, on the other.[18] Of course, in history, all precise boundaries are somewhat artificial. Prior to Descartes in the seventeenth century, a shift away from the medieval view of things had

16 The situation today is much more sophisticated but the nominalism of thought still prevails to a large degree. The physicist David Bohm and others have sought to free theoretical physics from the dominance of mechanism by focusing upon what he has called the "integral order" of the universe, but they remain a minority among theoretical physicists, though a suggestive one. And in recent biology there have been attempts to avoid the reduction of biology to the biochemistry of organisms.

17 Cf. David Hume's decisive insistence upon the discreteness of the sensory impressions, thus relegating the principle of causality to the imputation of the knower. Kant, too, placed the justification of necessary relations among ideas (and hence the possibility of scientific certitude) in the mind rather than in relations intrinsic to the things themselves.

18 Were I tracing the history of modern philosophy, I should have to deal in greater detail with the historical influences and circumstances of each thinker. Moreover, I should have to deal with the empiricist current, ranging from Locke through Hume and beyond. Since I am considering only the fundamental structure underlying the reduction of things (*res*) to objects, the empiricists add to the *content* of the conception of the object (an addition that Kant takes into consideration in his own way) but do not alter the logical structure of objects.

been under way for at least two centuries.[19] And after Kant in the nineteenth century, modern presuppositions have lingered even until our own times. For all that, however, Descartes and Kant do mark significant resting points in the development of Western philosophy, and illuminate what I have called the "death" of things. Between them they mark out the high-points of what might be called the "logic of modernity."

For a philosopher to stand out from among his peers, he must gather up issues left unresolved by past philosophical enquiry and, at the same time, show the way to new and compelling possibilities of thought. It is just this convergence of past and future that also recommends the philosopher's influence to the larger scene beyond the confines of philosophy. Descartes meets these twin demands brilliantly, and his influence can be found even today in a manner of thought that has effected a more or less current attitude towards nature and ourselves.

I have remarked upon the nominalism at work in Descartes's thought. It received new power when coupled with his famous methodical doubt: which was the determination to clear the mirror of the mind of all that it had inherited in the way of prior knowledge-claims, a sort of mental garbage removal. So pressing was this doubt that it did not rest until it had swept away everything but the existence of thought itself: *cogito ergo sum.* Not even the seeming solidity of things could escape the doubt. The doubt was a powerful dissolution of the stability of that cosmos which Cicero had found so secure. Moreover, the methodic doubt owes more to the sense of radical contingency introduced by biblical thought than it may have cared to admit.[20]

19 Descartes himself retained some medieval principles (largely through his Jesuit teachers, and particularly through the influence of Suarez's *Metaphysical Disputations*), though in a new context. See Étienne Gilson, *Index scholastico-cartésien* (Paris: Alcan 1912) and *Études sur le rôle de la pensée médiévale dans la formation du système cartésien* (Paris: Virin 1930). This is most noticeable in Descartes's proofs for the existence of God, and also in such discussions as that regarding the concept of triangularity. The idea of the triangular possesses a certain complex of properties (each of them: points, lines, angles, separate in themselves and related by distinct and external relations), but still, taken in itself as a whole, it is self-related and clearly distinct from other ideas.

20 Étienne Gilson observes in *The Philosopher and Theology* (trans. Cécile Gilson; New York: Random House 1962) that, while Descartes insists upon an allegedly "purely rational" philosophy devoid of all theological influence, the God of Descartes and his immediate followers looks markedly like the biblical God, a likeness that would have astounded the pre-Christian philosophers. As testament to the seriousness of such an idea of God, no one today who declared himself an atheist because he denied the existence of Zeus or Athena would be taken seriously. Modern atheism presupposes the biblical notion of God or some derivative therefrom. N.B.

It is significant that the sceptical instances offered by Descartes – the apparent brokenness of the stick half in and half out of the water, the tower whose apparent shape alters as we approach it – were not unknown to previous philosophers. Indeed, they were the stock-in-trade of earlier sceptics, bent upon denying the reliability of the senses; but they are scarcely decisive for the purpose to which Descartes put them. Given that Descartes was far from a dullard, we must look elsewhere for the patent inadequacy of the examples that are meant to feed the universal scope of such a doubt. Indeed, we find that they serve as window-dressing for a quite different proposal: a radically new proposal for understanding the role of thought and the way or method in which thought should be exercised. What Descartes has summed up and put his personal stamp upon is the general dissatisfaction among the learned with the older way of thought; and what he has set before his readers is the possibility of an unprecedented advance in thought. Of course, his own thought alone did not accomplish the full range of its objectives, but Descartes was the herald of the new way of approaching things and thought, a sort of John the Baptist to advancing rational thought.[21]

Nevertheless, Descartes's original insight into the power of methodic thought was subsumed into a larger and more complex development. For his legacy held within it several significant contributions to the shaping of the modern mind. The most obvious contribution was to render more explicit the demand for precision in thought. As already mentioned in respect to the logic of the given, the word "precise" rests upon the verb "to cut," as when a surgeon makes an "incision" or when we decide and thereby exclude other alternatives. The medieval Schoolmen had distinguished between the mental operation of abstraction and that of precision. Abstraction is essentially the non-consideration of other elements than that to which the mind attends in a given activity, as when it disregards the peculiarities of Socrates to attend to the fact that he is human and to what he shares with other human beings. Precision, on the other hand, is the act by which the mind actively prescinds from everything else and closes in on nothing but the essential structure attended to by the mind. For the Schoolmen, the contrast was between an open

21 Descartes's physics failed to convince others, and even his method was to be supplemented by empirical methods of enquiry at the hands of Locke and others, not to mention the empirical observations and the experiments of the scientists. In the eighteenth century, D'Alembert was to signal the compound of rational and empirical factors as the progressive movement of thought itself. See his *Preliminary Discourse to the Encyclopedia of Diderot* (Indianapolis, Ind.: Library of Liberal Arts).

abstraction vs/ precision

mental operation (abstraction) and a closed one (precision).[22] In its own way Descartes's method was one of precision. Here again we meet the nominalism present in Descartes's new method: to separate out each self-enclosed element of thought and to relate the separated elements by linking them one to another after the manner of those "long and easy chains of reasoning" familiar to geometers. This was not intended to reduce everything to mathematics but, quite the reverse, was intended to raise the method (only partially exploited by mathematics) to the universal method of correct reasoning (*mathesis universalis*).[23] Once in possession of true ideas, thought was not to penetrate them in the old way – by uncovering their intrinsic correlatedness within the original composite wholes (*res*) – but rather was to move from one idea and to connect it with another objectively, that is, as one connects (mental) objects.

The new method rested upon a dynamic introspection by which thought moved back towards and into itself: *cogito ergo sum.* Moving away from the purported unreliability of the sensory-based knowledge of things, thought moved back into itself to find there the only secure foundation for a renewed approach to the world. The partial distantiation already present in Greek conceptualization now ceased to be partial and became total; or to put it in medieval terms, abstraction gave way to precision. The famous dualism of Descartes – "I am *only* a thinking thing" (*res cogitans*), and "the external world is *nothing but* extension" (*res extensa*) – uses the medieval language of *res*, but it gives the term *res* a new meaning. Moreover, the separation of the two domains of thought and extension is not only the separation of mind and body but even more the separation of thought and world; so that the world disappears, so to speak, down Alice's rabbit hole until Descartes thinks that he has retrieved it (in the reduced state of pure extension) by the method of clear and distinct ideas and mathematical-like reasoning. It is important to clarify two consequences of this modern way of first separating and then

N.B.

22 In a note to his edition of Thomas Aquinas's *On Being and Essence* (Toronto: Pontifical Institute of Mediaeval Studies 1968), 39, Armand Maurer puts the distinction clearly: "Precision is a mode of abstraction by which we cut off or exclude something from a notion. Abstraction is the consideration of something without either including or excluding from its notion characteristics joined to it in reality. Abstraction without precision does not exclude anything from which it abstracts, but includes the whole thing, though implicitly and indeterminately."

23 Cf. the long reflection upon the *Vorverständnisse* which we are said to bring to things in the form of prior categories according to Martin Heidegger's interpretation of Kant's transcendental doctrine in *Die Frage nach dem Ding,* and which he seems to endorse in his own way.

re-establishing the relation of thought to world. The first consequence bears upon the character of the introversion, the second upon its impact on things. First, the movement of thought back into itself is quite different from the religious movement that only seems to resemble it. Modern Cartesian introspection moves away from a world with which it is dissatisfied for epistemic reasons: it holds that existing knowledge is dubious.[24] Descartes was concerned that the world as it presents itself to us does not seem to measure up to the demand for precision and certitude put upon it by the new way of thought. Such an attitude of thought could no longer be satisfied with the soft universality of the old way, which was content if the evidence held "for the most part" (*plerumque*). In the old way, any "exceptions" could be left to the more generous lap of being, whereas the newly empowered thought could tolerate none in its own demanding house. The new method sought absolute conformity to whatever rules thought devised: universality now came to mean "unexceptionality."[25] So demanding was the new way of thought that it could find no resting place in any other than itself. For, try as it might, thought could not deny that in the very effort to doubt all things – and pre-eminently, to doubt itself – thought was required to acknowledge its own existence.[26] In Heidegger's famous formula, human thought has become the *subjectum fundamentum inconcussum.* Modernity has received its formal seal: what is unshakeable is no longer the cosmos but the human subject.

A casual glance may not detect the radical difference between the new introspection and the older path of religious interiority. The religious movement within also begins with a sort of dissatisfaction with the world of things. It also withdraws into the recesses of the soul. It does this, however, not primarily for epistemic reasons, that is, in order to build a new and better scientific understanding, nor does it come to rest in the human *psyche* as the absolute foundation of certitude; but rather the soul moves within in order to join itself with the source of its hoped-for blessedness. Instead of coming to rest in the human mind, therefore, persons

24 In this sense, Cartesian reflection is a replay under modern conditions of the Greek distantiation. But the ancient expectation is more exploratory than critical and does not raise the demand for precision or introspection to such a uniform level. Nor is the distantiation absolute and total as Descartes intended it to be within the universal methodical doubt in methodically disengaging thought from anything except itself.

25 Universals in the older way held firm in the face of exceptions, whereas the generalities of the new way required a revision in the face of observed exceptions.

26 Without embracing Descartes's restrictive method, we may nonetheless see that, inasmuch as he is the advocate of the primacy of modern subjectivity, the French philosopher sets the stage for Hegel's more ambitious and capacious proposal (*Zumutung*) in the *Science of Logic* to carry out the project of "*absolutes Denken.*"

in religious prayer ask to be forgiven their transgressions in order to enter into communion with the source of their being which they have received as a gift. Far from resting everything upon the security of the self, they surrender that security to a greater Thou, so that they might come into the uplands of the spirit and place themselves before God as the source of their being and the term of their hope. In short, Cartesian introspection is not religious meditation.

A second, less obvious consequence of the modern transfer to the human subject is what happens to things. In the religious conversion, all things are ultimately offered up and returned to their Creator as gifts received. In the Cartesian reversion to the world, things are returned to the demands of the *res cogitans*, in conformity with the rules of the method. To be sure, Descartes finally returns to the world with the aid of a proof of God's existence, whose existence he thought to have proven beyond doubt. Subsequent developments proved otherwise, however, and even before his physics came under fire, his proofs of God came under attack. What is more important for the present theme, however, is what the reversion means for the understanding of things. For, although Descartes satisfied himself that he could return to the world, the recovery by way of method returned him to a quite different world from the one he had left as he turned within himself. What had become of the things of yesteryear? Instead of "thick" things with their own depth, Descartes returned to a world of thin extension, bearing the so-called primary qualities of quantity, extension, figure, dimensions, and size; that is, to the mathematical properties of extended objects. Instead of many finite composite substances, he returned to the one substance of pure extension.

Implied in this change, moreover, is that the things of nature have been turned into objects standing over against the mind. For those of us brought up in the modern mindset, nothing is more uncontroversial than that we are surrounded by a world of objects. Still, this would have seemed strange talk to earlier thinkers, and it is worth examining the logic inherent in the new attitude of objective thinking, for it reveals the nature of the shift to the new and modern way. To medieval thinkers, an object was not exactly a thing; it was the thing only insofar as it impinged upon the knowing faculties. The term "object" stood for a certain aspect, but not for the thing as a whole. Thus, a thing insofar as it reflected colour and had an impact on the eye was a visible object; the song of a bird insofar as it resounded in the ear was an audible object; and the soapy bar slipping away in the bath was a tangible object. In a word, an object was not simply a thing but only the way in which a thing impinged upon the sensory or mental faculties (*objectum formale*).

According to the older way, the thing was in itself not an object; it was a *subject*, a subject of being (*suppositum entis*). With the Cartesian revolution (though Descartes himself often used the older terminology while giving it a new content), the only subject was the human mind, the subject of thought *(subjectum mentis* and not *subjectum entis).* The pivotal point of the ancient Greek thought had been the *cosmos*, and of the medieval thinkers *theos*, but in the modern way promoted by Descartes the pivotal point was the *subjectum humanum*; if you will, *anthropos* conceived at first as mind or reason (Spinoza, Leibniz, Kant), or as passion (Hume), or later as will (Nietzsche). The things of nature are no longer understood to be members in the community of beings, creatures all, but primarily to be objects, standing over against human consciousness which is now the sole subject.

To be sure, this shift was intended to serve a noble ideal, nothing less than the improvement of the human condition. In a letter to his former teacher, which served as preface to the *Principles*, Descartes outlined the purposes of the revolution in thought. Using the metaphor of the tree of learning, Descartes compared the roots to metaphysics (philosophy as fundamental enquiry) and the trunk to physics (the general science of the physical world); but, he tells his reader, the fruits of knowledge lie at the end of the branches. The branches of the tree of knowledge are three, which we may translate into present-day terms as the practical sciences of medicine, engineering (or mechanics), and ethics. Empowered by the new method, these special sciences are intended to advance the "commodiousness" of mankind.[27]

This practical ideal was a commonplace among seventeenth-century philosophers, who, in different ways, sought to articulate the shift in the thought and in the practice that preceded it and to advance that shift along firm and fruitful lines. Francis Bacon held a similar ideal, seeking

27 The term (from the Latin *commodus*) bears the sense of "agreeably useful, suitable." This returns us under modern conditions to the earlier Greek term (*ta chrêmata*) instead of *ta onta*, or to the medieval *bonum utile.* This indicates a certain affinity with the pre-Socratic philosophers. Descartes and Bacon expressed a distinct preference for the earlier thinkers over Plato and Aristotle, for whom they held a vivid (if not a livid) antipathy. Cf. Heidegger's relegation of *ta onta* to the ontic level and his appeal to the earlier Greek philosophers. It is perhaps significant that the critique of Plato and Aristotle's ontology occurred in the seventeenth century, which formulated the paradigm of modernity, and in the twentieth, which, at least since Heidegger, began to destruct or deconstruct modernity. In criticism of the modern ideal, a group of philosophers as diverse as Marcel and Adorno have characterized the ideal as having degenerated to the provision of commodities.

to empower knowledge with the means of exploiting nature to the benefit of mankind, though there is more of the older attitude evident in his thought.[28] Hobbes, too, tells us that previously among the Scholastics, the field of knowledge was too little cultivated, so that only a few acorns grew in those barren fields of subtle speculation, whereas with the application of a new method (Hobbes thought almost exclusively in terms of applied geometry) a rich harvest could be had. Bacon and Hobbes, even more than Descartes, bring out the practical motive of the modern revolution: that man should become master of the world about him, a possibility brought closer to realization by the increase in technical inventions and the growing power of technology.

What is new here is not that knowledge is power, or even that knowledge has the power to produce results.[29] What is new is the pre-eminent motive proposed for the investigation of nature: the practical, or rather the productive, result tended to render theoretical knowledge subservient to it.[30]

Immersed in thought as it was, the new attitude, particularly in the new sciences, did not abandon the world of nature; on the contrary, it forged a new definition of physical reality that met the standards of an objectivism based on the new attitude. And so it brought to its investigations an intense scrutiny into the workings of nature. What was new, then, were the values that it sought in nature. These were the values of the ideal of objectivity which the Cartesian version of the new way and

28 *Novum Organum*, 192. To his famous dictum that "human knowledge and power coincide, for ignorance of cause deprives one of the effect," he immediately adds that "nature to be commanded must be obeyed." This stands in contrast to Descartes's third rule of method in the *Discourse*, to the effect that, if one cannot find grounds for ordering ideas in the ideas themselves, one should impose an order upon them, since lack of order is to be avoided at all costs. The idealization inherent in mathematics undoubtedly made such a suggestion more commendable to Descartes.

29 In the *Proemium* to his *Commentary on the Metaphysics of Aristotle*, St Thomas insists that *all* knowledge is for the sake of a resultant end, namely, human happiness. That end differs, however, from the seventeenth-century ideal insofar as Thomas defines happiness in terms of a state of being rather than in terms of the attainment of commodiousness produced through mastery of nature. We see here the grounds for Gabriel Marcel's distinction between *being* and *having*.

30 Even here, however, we find ambiguity; for Bacon writes that "works are to be undertaken insofar as they are pledges of truth rather than insofar as they contribute to the comfort of life." (*Novum Organum* 329.) As already mentioned, Hobbes is much less nuanced, complaining that the pursuit of some theoretical issue is not worth the labour of thought to master it. To him, the proper issue of thought is some product. (*De corpore* I.)

the burgeoning sciences of physics and optics rendered in terms of quantitative and/or statistical correlations.[31] Instead of seeking in nature for ultimate causes and principles, as the *via antiqua* had done, the new way sought the precise formulation of the behaviour of physical elements in accordance with mathematically expressed laws. The new interplay between thought and production, under the ideal of a mastery that would improve the material condition of humankind and so liberate humanity in unprecedented ways, was confirmed in the eighteenth century by an industrial revolution that was fuelled by a prodigious increase in technological power and control. Despite the success it has achieved on its own terms, however, the ideal of an objective science of nature that claims to be value-neutral stands in need of further scrutiny. It is not that the metaphysical approach is value-laden (and hence subjective), while the objective approach is value-empty and neutral; but rather that each approach seeks values in nature, although quite different ones.

Moreover, the new approach contains within it another salient feature. That feature is well stated by Descartes: "There is only one human wisdom, *quae semper una et eadem manet*, which always remains one and the same; it suffers no more differentiation from its application to different objects than the light of the sun is affected by the differences amongst the objects on which it shines ... In a word, there is *a single and identical method* to be applied to each and every field of knowledge – a method discovered hitherto only in mathematics but ultimately reflecting

N.B.

31 Cf. John Burbidge, *Being and Will* (New York: Paulist Press 1977), chapter 5, "The Authority of Reason," esp. 46ff.: "The science of statistical correlation no less than reflection on qualitative characteristics [unlike the "logic of the will"] abstracts from existent actuals, and uses ideas and concepts to articulate possibilities. In doing so, however, it regards quantities as the essential characteristics because they relate, free from qualitative ambiguity. Magnitude, shape and number are common to all spatio-temporal entities and provide a universal basis for comparison. Quantities, therefore, are the essential traits while qualities are accidental. This criterion of what is necessary is the universal presupposition of all science. Modern science, no less than medieval, is concerned with relations that are not simply spatial or temporal. In their most primitive forms these will be correlations of quantity." This astute observation holds particularly for the modern mathematization of science. Medieval science did not hold that quantities are any less accidental than qualities; instead, it held to an analogical basis respectful of specific differences among things rather than to a univocal and uniform quantitative one. In short, medieval science was grounded in substances and their relations rather than primarily in quantitative relations.

the very nature of human reason itself."[32] It is not too much to claim that Western culture drew many of its best minds into the project of modernity formulated by Descartes, and with stunning results. More detailed examination of the subsequent interplay between thought and production belongs to the history of technology, but early modern philosophy formulated the ideal of a mastery that would improve the material condition of humankind along the path of objective research, thus accomplishing the liberation of humanity from much servile labour. That liberation was verified in the very progress of inventions and their application, and it received the name of "progress." To the modern project there belonged three features: an ideal (the commodiousness of mankind), a value (the mathematical quantities of nature), and a uniform method (modelled upon mathematical reasoning). All of this rested upon the primacy of rational thought centred in the human subject armed with the method and techniques of control.

Nor did this profound change in the human condition affect only the devising of new products for the comfort of mankind. More sweeping consequences accompanied the change: above all, a new sense of individuality emerged, which was reflected in the spheres of politics, economics, and social relations. That new sense of individuality was celebrated and promoted, as Hegel has shown, by the "prophets" of the new way who were themselves not integrated into the established institutions of the existing society.[33] The new approach received its political and social expression in the form of classical liberalism. Scholars debate whether there is a necessary connection between liberalism and

32 *Regulae ad directionem ingenii* (*Oeuvres* X, 359). Developments in the sciences introduced a strong empirical evidence into the enquiry (as both the Encyclopedists and Kant recognized), but this did not alter the logic of the method fundamentally. Although Pascal in the seventeenth century criticized the Cartesian "spirit of geometry," it was not until the early eighteenth century that Vico (*Scienza nuova*) initiated the recognition that historical enquiry needed a different method than the uniform Cartesian method modelled upon mathematics. Such a recognition had been implicit since the Greeks "invented" the historical account, but it had been obscured in the early modern period by the dominance of Cartesian mathematicism.

33 Cf. Hegel, *Phenomenology of Spirit*, chapter 6. Among the intellectual leaders it has been noticed that none of the most influential philosophers held official positions in the universities, neither Descartes, nor Spinoza, nor Leibniz, nor Bacon, nor Hobbes, nor Hume, nor even Locke (Kant was the first, from 1755); nor among the popularizers, Diderot, D'Alembert, Voltaire, Rousseau, Condorcet. It is not incidental, then, that they addressed their appeals either to the rational, passional, or volitional element in the individual.

capitalism.[34] But there can be no doubt that a heightened sense of individuality functions in both, so that while liberalism can take different modern political forms (such as libertarianism or neo-conservatism), the primary ideal of individual freedom is inherent in each of them. Of course, the value of freedom was not absent from earlier periods of our culture; indeed, it received contributions even from biblical religion; yet a value is not quite an ideal, and it is beyond doubt that the modern shift to the *subjectum humanum* as central to thought and action gave a heightened value to the ideal of freedom in its individual form.

N.B Of especial interest in this regard is the prevalent use in the seventeenth century of the Latin term *conatus* to express the tendency of the will.[35] Earlier discussions of the will in medieval thought had, following Aristotle, tied the will rather closely to the *teleology* of the good – first of all, to the universal good (with the Scholastics, *bonum transcendentale*), then to the specifically human good (*bonum honestum*), and finally in the various situations of life to particular goods meant to complete the human good (including *bonum utile*). *Conatus*, on the other hand, does not lay stress on the finality of the will but rather on its efficacy. We may not be surprised to find the brusque Hobbes asserting that the right of nature "is the liberty each man hath, to use his own power as he will himself, for the preservation of his own nature".[36] It is perhaps more surprising that the "gentle" Spinoza gives a kind of canonical formulation of the notion of the will as *conatus*,[37] saying that

every individual has sovereign right to do all that he can; in other words, *the rights of an individual extend to the utmost limits of his power as it has been conditioned.* Now, it is the sovereign law and right of nature that each individual should endeavour to preserve itself as it is, *without regard to anything but itself*; therefore this sovereign law and right belongs to every individual, namely, to exist and act

34 See the discussion in John A. Hall, *Liberalism: Politics, Ideology and the Market* (Chapel Hill: North Carolina University Press 1987), 35–62 and passim).

35 For a more adequate textual basis, see my essay "Is Liberalism Good Enough?" in R. Bruce Douglass *et al.*, ed., *Liberalism and the Good* (New York Routledge 1990), 86–104, esp. 89–91.

36 *Leviathan* I, 14. He also asserts the famous dictum that in the state of nature "every man hath a right to everything; even to another's body." Moreover, unlike Thomas Aquinas, who defined law as an ordinance of reason, Hobbes designates it as "deed enforced," sometimes called the "principle of effectivity."

37 *A Political Treatise*, chapter 2, sec. 3–5. The rejection of final causality (at the end of Book I of the *Ethics*) is of the same cloth as his notion of *conatus*.

according to its natural conditions ... As the wise man has sovereign right to do all that reason dictates ... so also the ignorant and foolish man has sovereign *right* to do *all that desire dictates.*[38]

To be sure, such *conatus* was moderated by various conditions, such as the co-existing power of others and the dictates of interest. What is significant, however, is that the status of *rights* is attributed even to the inordinate use of *conatus.*

In more moderate but still vigorous terms, Descartes also underscores the pre-eminent range of the will: "[God] has given me a volition more ample than my understanding. For as the volition consists of just one body, [its subject being] apparently indivisible, it seems that its nature is such that nothing could be taken from it without destroying it."[39] Here Descartes proclaims the disjunct: either absolutely free or not free at all, which was to become the dichotomy: determinism or indeterminism. This dichotomy differs from the medieval qualified form of freedom which situated it within and tailored it to the end inherent in the nature of each thing. In declaring the human understanding to be finite and the human will to be infinite (because simple and indivisible),[40] Descartes released the will in principle from the teleology in which it had been embedded by Aristotle and his medieval descendants. Instead, Descartes endorsed the late medieval thesis of the will's absolute indifference to every alternative, an indifference that coincided with its infinitude. This contributed in no small measure to the eventual separation of will and intellect, of thought and action, so tightly bound together in the classical medieval exposition by Thomas Aquinas.[41]

But this emphasis upon the primacy of the will, already discernible in late medieval thought, had also received endorsement in Renaissance terms with Pico della Mirandola's famous fable, according to which, in

38 *A Theological-Political Treatise,* chapter 16, in *The Works of Spinoza,* trans. R.H.M. Elwes, 2 vols. (New York: Dover 1951), 1:292, 200 (emphasis added).

39 From the fourth Meditation in *The Meditations on First Philosophy,* vol. 2 of *The Philosophical Writings of Descartes* (Cambridge, U.K.: Cambridge University Press 1984). Insofar as he endorses the "liberty of indifference," at least as the lowest grade of freedom, Descartes does not stress the conative act of the will as do some of his immediate followers, but he does nullify any teleology of the good.

40 *Meditations* IV: "I am conscious of a will so extended as to be subject to no limits."

41 For another view, see the critical reflections of John Burbidge (*Being and Will,* especially chapter 5, "The Authority of Reason"), to the effect that finality presupposes a (to him, questionable) isomorphism between the categories of reason and the activity of things. It seems to me, however, that it is just this imperfect "isomorphism" that warrants the possibility of the exercise of our freedom in the understanding of things.

creating the world, God had given to each being a well-defined specific nature. When he came to create man, however, God found that he had no more finite natures to give out. Instead, he gave to man freedom. Moreover, that freedom had a divine correlate, for it was not in man's intellect but in his will that the image of God in man is to be found.[42]

As with so many fundamental concepts, the term "freedom" is understood in a variety of different ways. Even with those meanings of freedom that only differ but do not contradict one another, the variety is dependent upon the aspect featured in function of the interest of the enquirer. This is attributable not so much to the vagueness of the concept as to its rich intelligibility and profound importance for human existence. Like a diamond with many facets, the eye of the mind is caught now by one facet, now by another, as a different light is brought to shine upon it. Thus, we speak sometimes of freedom *from*, claiming a certain independence and liberation; at another, we recognize the opening to opportunity and initiative, as freedom *to*; and at still other times, we acknowledge a call to serve and speak of freedom *for*.

In a more conceptually developed manner, three explicit understandings of freedom are relevant to our present topic regarding a more adequate appreciation of things. The first and older understanding is the teleological and appetitive concepts of freedom: as that by which we seek (*ad-peto*) the good as our end (*telos*). In the Platonic and Aristotelian traditions, as well as in the medieval, freedom was by its inherent nature ordered towards the good – for Plato this was the supreme form of the Good, for Aristotle it was above all the political good, that is, participation in a fully human life within the *polis*. Undergirding this orientation was a sense of cosmic order. Within this cosmic order, human beings were to find their proper good, the *bonum honestum*, which was meant to take precedence over both the good of pleasure (*bonum delectabile*) and the merely useful (*bonum utile*). This sense of a primordial orientation was reinforced by the Christian doctrine of creation and providence, whereby God gives to each thing its own nature with a built-in intended good, such as its own preservation or the continued renewal of its kind. In creating man, God endowed him with an intelligent nature having the capability for knowledge and deliberative freedom. In the words of Thomas Aquinas: man has dominion over his own actions. The distinctive character of human freedom is that it is not determined to one outcome but rather is able to engage its knowledge in a process

42 Lobkowicz (*Thoery and Practice*, 136–7) lodges the earliest expression of a "denatured freedom" with Ficino (1474).

of deliberation, choice, and enactment (*liberum arbitrium*). This calls for a just and wise dealing with the Creator, with other persons, and with other things through the cultivation and formation of the relevant virtues (or "strengths"). Although free to act autonomously, according to this understanding of freedom, the human being is oriented or inclined – but not pre-determined – by its nature and origin towards the finality of an absolute Good – namely, communion with God.

In the seventeenth century, however, the most influential philosophers (Descartes and Spinoza, Bacon and Hobbes[43]) all rejected final causality and sought the good closer to home in the commodiousness of ordinary life. No doubt this rejection of finality in nature prepared the way for a different concept of freedom, which we might call *formal* freedom in contrast to *teleological* freedom. It was Kant who gave canonical expression and formulation to this understanding. For him, freedom was realized, not simply in freedom from heteronomy, from submission to others,[44] but in the purely rational motivation of a self-legislating Reason. What was to be eschewed was the teleological dynamic which the classical and medieval notion had endorsed. In Kant's eyes, to admit any considerations of the good – other than the purely rational apprehension of one's duty and the universal applicability of the maxim guiding one's action – was to introduce sensory appetities that diminished the purity of the moral act. It was this aversion to conceding moral value to desires and emotions that, no doubt, led Kant to the various formulations of the absolutely binding (categorical) imperative: so act that your action in similar circumstances is universally valid for all rational agents; and the further formulation: so act that you treat persons, not simply as means [to your desires] but as ends in themselves. The respect for persons, originating in the Christina debates of the late classical and the medieval period, is now placed in a new, formal, and anthropological context.

The rejection of final causality[45] in the seventeenth century was part of a wholesale rejection or redefinition of the other causes that were part of the fabric of medieval metaphysics. Matter or material cause

43 To be precise, Bacon did not reject final causes outright, but he denied that they operated in subhuman reality, thus restricting finality to human purpose.

44 Although this is the principal theme of his more popular essay, *What Is Enlightment?*

45 There can be no doubt that the general reliance upon mathematics, elevated to first science with such fruitful experimental results in the study of nature, played a role in the dismissal of final causes, inasmuch as mathematics is both a formal and an ideal science. Unlike Aristotelian empirical biology, in which immediate intrinsic purposes can be discerned from the study of animal behaviour, any finality ascribed to mathematical operations must be introduced from another source.

(*'ulê, materia*) had been merely the principle that safeguarded the possibility of physical change (matter as potentiality to receiving form); it was now restricted to basic elemental particles. Form (*morphê, eidos, forma*) had been the principle determinative of the natures inherent in things, but now became – not the originative principle of order – but the end result of the laws of nature and was viewed as structure or design, that is as the result of priori elements and not their origin. And effective casuality (*causa efficiens*), which in the older view was the cause of being, now came to be understood as impetus, which initiated motion. What had been the origin of motion now became its starter.[46]

The third version of freedom (*conatus*) replaced the teleological version in the influential circles of seventeenth- and eighteenth-century thought, and even later received expression through Nietzsche's "Will to Power" and, more recently still, through Jean-Paul Sartre's identification of freedom with antecedent choice. The emergence of this conative version of freedom can be traced to much earlier developments. Indeed, in later medieval circles associated with nominalism, a distinction was drawn between the divine *potentia absoluta* and the *potentia ordinata*, that is, between God's absolute power and that more limited version which he effected in creating a finite world. With the shift to the human subject as unshakeable centre and foundation (*inconcussum fundamentum*), it was not a large step to transfer the concept of absolute freedom from the divine to the human, especially with the emergence in the eighteenth century not so much of atheism as of a growing secularism, that is of the displacement of the sacred by the human.[47] One of the decisive moves that dissociated freedom from its rational embedding in the cosmos (*communitas rerum*) is to be seen among those theologians who came under the influence of the great Persian philosopher Avicenna (*Ibn Sina*). As early as the thirteenth century, Matthew Cardinal Aquasparta had held that philosophy dealt with pure essences (*quidditates tantum*), and that only theology could address really existing things.[48] This withdrawal of

46 See my "Analysis by Principles and Analysis by Elements," in L. Gerson ed., *Graceful Reason: Essays in Ancient and Mediaeval Philosophy Presented to Joseph Owens CSSR* (Toronto: Pontifical Institute of Mediaeval Studies 1983), 315–30.

47 It is not accidental that Descartes, by no means a nominalist theologian, holds in the *Meditations on First Philosophy* that, while the mind in the possession of its ideas is finite, the human will is infinite.

48 In the seventeenth century, the Oratorian and Augustinian Nicolas Malebranche, under the influence of Cartesian doubt, seems to have taken up a similar position, relying on Genesis, that is, on divine revelation, for the definitive confirmation of the existence of the world: "To deliver you entirely from your speculative [Cartesian] doubt, faith furnishes us a demonstration which it is impossible to resist." (*Entretiens sur la Métaphysique* 6, 8; cited in Copleston, *A History of Philosophy*, bk. 2, vol. 4: 198.)

philosophical reflection from the existing world, no doubt, contributed to dislodging the understanding of freedom from the fabric of things. One expression of this disengagement, differing among different thinkers, is that which describes human freedom as consisting entirely of the "liberty of indifference" between two alternative possible choices.

Along with the growing interest in the study of motion for its own sake, this dislodgement from the fabric of the context of causes, including final causality – that is, the dislodgment from freedom understood within the context of an order of created goods – led to a stress on freedom as the absolute origination of action, an understanding that is perhaps a dominant concept of freedom in liberal Western thought today. One finds the notion of *conatus* expressed in Spinoza, understood as the original dynamism that constitutes the very essential nature of action. Leibniz, too, endorsed the notion of an innate active tendency (*vis activa*) on the part of the monads. Even earlier, the study of motion had begun to take this phenomenon as self-given. Motion in general and as such thus became a first principle that explained everything in the physical world without itself needing an explanation. This stood in contrast with the earlier metaphysical view of motion as an imperfect modality that needed to be understood through causes that transcended motion. Eventually, of course, Newton crowned this several-centuries' long effort with his descriptive study of the general laws of motion. The mind then turned away from causal enquiry and more towards the precise description of the interaction of particles in accord with the laws of motion.[49] Explanation by appeal to ontological causes gave way to description by way of forces and laws.

As we survey these various understandings of freedom, the question arises whether we can embrace these different versions in a new synthesis? I think that we can. And it is this synthesis that I would call "the new freedom." What is new in modernity is not only the emphasis upon the conative aspect of freedom, the energy of choice and self-determination, but also the developed appreciation of the value of freedom itself. We see this not only in the experimental verve of science but also in the modern novel, in abstract art, and in new social arrangements. I have already compared freedom to a many-faceted diamond, and I think that each of the three versions of freedom (appetitive or teleological, normative or formal, and conative or initiative) draws attention to one or another

49 See the earlier reference to Gaukroger, *Descartes* (Oxford, U.K.: Clarendon 1995), 70–2, above at 53n17, as well as the prior discussion of *conatus* at 65, 72–3. The demand for the atomic description of motion belongs to the same presuppositions that lay the foundation for the conative view of freedom. Such atomism was, of course, not unknown previously among the ancient Greeks, but in that earlier period it was placed within an ontological context.

facet. The framework for the resolution of these differences, however, is provided by the traditional metaphysics of causal principles. For each version stems from one of the causes: the appetitive from final causality, the normative from formal causality, and conative from effective causality. It seems to me that the difference is not one of contradiction but of complementarity and that we need them all both for the understanding of action and for properly human action itself.

Freedom in search of the good that will perfect the human agent is extolled by the first version, the teleological dynamic of the will inclinded towards the good. Yet, although inclined towards the good (anticipated in the received nature of the agent: Aristotle's *entelechy*), the will is capable of setting aside one good for another, real or apparent, out of concern for some other interest, perhaps more immediate; for example, the *bonum delectabile* or the *bonum utile* is chosen rather than the *bonum honestum.* This facet of freedom is expressed negatively by the notion of the liberty of indifference, which enunciates the freedom of the will in the face of alternative choices. The effective originating power of the will to move itself is illuminated positively by the notion of *conatus.* Indeed, I take the liberty of indifference and *conatus* to be two sides of freedom understood as indeterminacy – the former being a negative expression of that indeterminacy, the latter a positive assertion of it. Finally, the normative character of properly human action is expressed ontologically by the concept of natural law as inherent in human nature and human freedom (the teleological version) and also deontically within the human reason by Kant's formalism of obligation and duty.

The conflict between these versions arises over the proper hierarchy and primacy of one or another version. Thus, if we understand freedom as principally *conative,* we understand ourselves to be free, antecedent to all considerations: as Spinoza says, as far as our power may extend; or as Sartre says, prior to the conferral of value which comes about alone by virtue of our act of choice. Underlying this understanding of freedom is the shift to the absolute primacy of the subject, in Spinoza in the context of power, in Sartre in the context of decision. This receives expression in today's culture in such maxims as Bella Abzug's: "It does not matter *what* you choose! It only matters *that* you choose!" or – during elections – "It doesn't matter how you vote as long as you vote"; or more concisely still, "Just do it!!" Unfortunately, it does matter what we do, how we vote; and so the other facets are indispensable. Things start to go wrong with our freedom when we separate these various aspects and divorce them from one another. Each has a part to play in an integral freedom. The conative liberty of indifference throws the exercise of our freedom back upon ourselves as our responsibility, just because we are free and not coerced. This version discloses the root indeterminacy of freedom. The formal, rule-governed version provides the determinacy that should govern our free acts, not as an external imposition but as intrinsic to the very character of freedom. Finally, the orientation to the good insisted upon by the teleological and eudaimonic concept of freedom – its relation to the human good and the good of the world – grounds that normed responsibility by giving it a determinate character in relation to the good within the context of the community of beings. All three understandings enter into the constitution of the new integral freedom.

No doubt, the modern emphasis falls upon the conative liberty of indifference, upon indeterminacy and self-determination, and these are precious values, greatly appreciated and developed in the modern era. It is undeniable that modern Western thought has raised this facet to a prominence that is unprecedented. But, as in so much of human development, it has often been at the cost of losing the broader and deeper context in which we are called upon to discharge a fuller freedom. It seems to me that this deeper context needs to include, not only our own proper and immediate good, defined by the centrality of the human subject and the human will, but the good of things as well, since they are our companions on the way and neighbours with whom we need to realize our freedom. It is through an integration of the conative with the teleological and the normative facets of freedom that we become "good citizens" of the world.

We have now before us the basic features of the modern outlook in its classical seventeenth-century formulation. This profile set the pattern for subsequent thought: with the inversion of thought over being, things had lost their status as subjects. This is an important loss, for, at least since the Middle Ages, we have usually reserved the term "subject" for what is fundamental in our scale of values. Instead, with the inversion characteristic of the logic of modernity, things became objects over against the only remaining subject, the only determinant of the way things are to be known with certitude; and this determinant is the human subject. The modern reservation of the status of subject to the human psyche, coupled with the strength of will enshrined in the notion of *conatus*, gives the *rationale* to man's aggressive conquest of nature. Nature now becomes the field of manipulable materials, in the interest of the commodiousness of mankind. The biblical command to become stewards of nature under God becomes the call to absolute mastery of nature.[50] Many other factors intervened in this transition, and they would have to be considered in any full account, but the logic of modernity has remained consistent. The eighteenth century reflected the growing empiricism incorporated into the progress of scientific enquiry, but the logic remains the same. To see this, we need only turn to Kant, who marks a decisive boundary in the development of modern thought.

In the preface to the second edition of the *Critique of Pure Reason,* Kant expresses most clearly the dynamism of his critical philosophy. Surprisingly, his criticism of the Scholastics was not principally that, as Bacon had averred, they were too abstract, but, on the contrary, that they were too closely wed to Nature.[51] Their fault was that they accepted everything that Nature presented to them uncritically, following after it as a child tied to its mother's apron strings. The innovation that put the study of Nature upon the secure path of a science was the recognition that Reason must not simply observe Nature, accepting whatever it appears to present, but rather that Reason must constitute itself a judge and, calling Nature into the witness box, demand of it that it answer questions drawn up a priori after a plan of Reason's own devising. To be sure, empirical observation is also needed, for, having called Nature to answer, Reason must not simply attend to itself. Reason must listen to Nature, but not to everything it has to say. For it is up to Reason, in its search for certitude, to set the conditions for what will count as significant and acceptable evidence.[52]

Here we see the Cartesian understanding enthroned as the Kantian critic of Nature, the human subject as ultimate determinant of what counts, not only as valid evidence, but also as what is significant and worthy of serious attention. But a price must be paid: dreams of a metaphysical knowledge of real things must be given up. Instead, the inherent logic of modern objectivity must be acknowledged and put in the place of honour. Kant differs from his idealistic predecessors in that knowing for him is referential, relation to objects, and not mental possession of

50 In the political field this sets up the alternatives of liberalism and statism, for the will is understood to lie in the political subject, which in liberalism is understood to be the individual and in statism the collective. Modern politics has wavered between these two inseparable poles ever since, as politicians take a position on the extreme right or extreme left or somewhere in-between. What is needed is the polarity not of individual or collective, but rather of person and community.

51 It is clear that we are no longer talking about things as members participating in a community of being, but of Nature gathered up into a totality that is set over against the human mind as a system of objects.

52 Kant, *Critique of Pure Reason,* 2d ed., Preface, B xii–xiv.

ideas.[53] As things give way to objects, the enquiring subject plays a double role. On the one hand, in the relation that constitutes the knowing of objects (and that was later to be termed "intentionality"), Reason stands over against the objects, as one party (the empirical subject or *ego*) to the relation between subject and object. But, on the other hand, Reason also plays a totalizing and rule-setting role (the transcendental subject or *ego*), for it sets the conditions under which the material of sensation can arrive at the desired standard of objectivity.

Kant recognized the ambiguous and incomplete status of the object as it had proceeded from the Cartesian revolution. For if the object was, in a sense, the shape of knowledge constructed in accordance with the "essential needs" of reason, then it could not claim the full-bodied being associated with the earlier sense of things. If the material of knowledge could appear only under the actively determining conditions of the knowing subject, objects had now received a further emptying: they were no longer that which stands over against the mind as objects (with a diminished, residual independence), but that which appears to the mind as phenomena, under the mind's conditions; that is, they were in effect appearances not things. Come, then, like good Kantians, let us sit upon the a priori ground of transcendental subjectivity and talk about the death of things.

It would be a mistake, however, to think that the Kantian philosophy had arrogated to itself the creative powers of God. In our effort to describe the Kantian revolution, we sometimes speak of the mind "fashioning" the phenomenal objects of knowledge, but such language misses the *differentia specifica* of Kant's critical idealism, which brings to completion the aim of philosophy from Descartes through to Kant. It is not accidental that epistemology now replaces metaphysics as the arch-science during the modern period, and that creation ceases to be considered seriously as a philosophical notion. For what is at issue in this modern period is not the attempt to replace the Creator God with a human creator; that happens as a by-product. What is at issue is not the coming into being of things at all, but rather the basis for justified knowledge-claims made by the human subject. What Kant seeks, and what Descartes sought before him, are the grounds for the validation of scientific knowledge, so that knowledge can meet the demands of scientific rigour, precision, and certitude. What is at stake is not the origination of

53 In the early modern period, knowing was understood to be the possession of rational ideas, as with Descartes, Spinoza, Leibniz, and Locke, or as the possession of sensory impressions, as with Hume.

beings but the justification of knowledge-claims; what is at stake is not the reality of things but the authority of the knower. The issue is not ontological constitution but epistemic validation. This justification is achieved by Kant on the basis of a priori categories, but with a further bleaching out of the "thick" sense of things. For things are translated from objects in the early modern sense into phenomena in the sense of Kant's critical idealism. In keeping with these demands, the sphere of freedom has to be divorced from the field of cognition. Kant puts it thus: that knowledge has had to be limited in order to make room for (rational) faith. Hence the first *Critique* is followed by a second, the *Critique of Practical Reason,* which addresses the character of freedom in non-cognitive terms.

Transformed "things" have lost their relative independence. Loosely related to one another by external relations, they have entered into the bondage of system. The classical statement of this double shift is undoubtedly Kant's *architectonic* in the penultimate chapter of the *Critique of Pure Reason.* There he tells us that a philosophical system must fulfil the "essential needs of reason." As he names them, these needs are *cognitive* (What can I know?), *moral* (What ought I to do?), and *religious* (What may I hope?) The modern sense of system is of a totality whose units are defined essentially by their membership in the system. The looseness of the external relations permitted the surprise of discovery through empirical observation and theoretical innovation, while the totality itself sequestered a place within which such discovery could occur and be integrated. It is ironical but not surprising that, just as we are experiencing increased interdependence in reality, several quarters of contemporary thought have mounted an attack upon the very *idea* of system whose more rigorous features are today almost universally rejected.[54]

To pause in summary: we have come a long distance in our story of the thing. Two salient points have emerged. First, among the Greeks we have observed the shift from usables (*ta chrêmata*) and actionables (*ta pragmata*) to beings (*ta onta*). A broad and deep sense of the good (in the poetic form of a just order, *dikê*) pervaded Greek thought. Plato's and Aristotle's breathtaking shift expanded the horizon of being and

54 I have in mind not only such postmodern philosophers as François Lyotard but also existentialists, personalists, and ontologists such as Heidegger as well as ordinary language philosophers such as Austin. The fear with some, such as Lyotard, is that the ideal of system as totality tends towards the realization of totalitarian regimes, with consequent human wreckage. Despite the explicit rejection of system, however, the fundamental pre-eminence of the human condition is still operative in much of postmodern thought, if not in the form of subjectivity then in the context of language.

brought the mythical and cosmic sense of value within that horizon, thus recognizing the absolute value of the good. The cosmos remained as value-bearing as it had been in the cosmogony of poetic myth and in the cosmology of the earlier philosophers. Plato remarked upon the decisive character of the good which he held to be pre-eminent over other aspects of reality. With telling insight he observed that, while we may be satisfied with an approximately true account of what is really the case, we are not at all satisfied with what is only apparently good, we want the real thing and no substitute.[55] An *ersatz* good is no good at all. This points to the inherent power of the good, which, with Plato, has been expanded beyond the concern for justice, and even for right order. The good has been expanded to become the absolute and pre-eminent determinant, and points to the beginnings of the notion of the transcendental properties of being that are resident in things. Thus, we return to the metaphysical vision of the omnipresent features of being, which are meant to secure a foothold in the real (*ens*), an intelligible light for the knower (*verum*), an attraction that does not coerce our freedom (*bonum*), and a fullness that shines with glory (*pulchrum*).[56] But with the death of things, the transcendental good and its fellows are sent down into the philosopher's Sheol, there to dwell as the shades of memory in the abode of the dead. And so freedom loses its hold on being and seeks a new form. The issue of the good places before us the issue of the new freedom and its relation to things.

55 *Republic* 505d, 508e: "In the case of just and beautiful things, many people are content with what are believed to be so, even if they aren't really so, and they act, acquire, and form their own beliefs on that basis. However nobody is satisfied to acquire things he merely believes to be good, but everyone wants the things that *really are* good and disdains those that are merely believed to be so ... So that what gives truth to the things known and the power to know to the knower is the form of the good." And at 509b: "You should also say that not only do the objects of knowledge owe their *being known* to the good, but their *being* is also due to it."

56 Hans Urs von Balthasar, in *The Glory of the Lord* (Edinburgh: T. and T. Clark 1982; English trans., vol. 2), expresses this sense of order: "In the beginning there is [the beauty of] form: '*Im Ursprung ist Urform.*'"

4

The Things of Yesteryear and the New Freedom

> Liberty consists in doing what one desires
> J.S. Mill

> The only liberty I mean,
> is a liberty connected with order
> Edmund Burke

THE PREVIOUS CHAPTER traced the bleaching out of the density of things, of their depth and internal constitution, as they passed in the modern mind from things to objects to phenomena, the latter even now undergoing further deconstruction by some postmodern philosophers. The first chapter set a recent signpost in this development by quoting Bertrand Russell's relegation of the thing to a mental construction. Of course, there is much that could be said about the further developments after Kant, but with him we have reached a decisive limit-point in our story of the ontological structure of the thing.

I should like, then, to dwell somewhat upon Kant's significance, which far outreach the German educated public and the lecture halls frequented by students of philosophy. His influence in the German-speaking world was explosive. Shortly after a popular presentation of his critical idealism had appeared, enthusiasm knew no bounds. A "fan" (if the word is contracted from "fanatic," we are entitled to use it here) tried to put the first *Critique* to verse, and another proclaimed that if Jesus himself had sat at the feet of the professor from Königsberg he would have learned what he had tried to say. A merchant locked himself up in a hotel room for several days in Holland, his meals ordered in, while he tried to decipher the crabbed German text. A native German reader said he would have gotten farther if he had not run out of fingers with which to keep track of the relative pronouns strewn throughout the long convoluted sentences. Earlier, Kant had been known to be capable of an easy style – he was dubbed the *galant Magister* – but the arduous struggle to articulate the logic of modernity eventually prevailed. Even so, public enthusiasm came to overlook, if not to forgive, the intricacies of his prose. As with Abelard before him, wandering scholars came from all parts of the continent to the remote Baltic seaport to seek Kant out. The Catholic bishop of Würzburg sent his most promising priest to study under the great master.

To be sure, he was not without his critics. His sometime student Johann Herder, concerned with the effect the new philosophy was having upon the formation of Protestant ministers, complained that, in order to put a new thinker on his feet, it was not necessary to set all others on their heads. Not surprisingly perhaps, Kant did not fare so well in England. At the close of the eighteenth century (1797), a public subscription for lectures on Kant's philosophy failed in London for want of subscribers. Sometime later, the English philosopher John Stuart Mill and the French positivist August Comte held an exchange about the new revolutionary philosophy. At issue was whether it was worth the study of the difficult language of German in order to read the new philosophers who followed upon Kant, namely, Fichte, Schelling, and Hegel. To the question the reply was given: No! It was not worth the trouble to read them, but it was worth the trouble to learn German in order to read Goethe. Some interest was generated by Coleridge upon his return from studies in Germany, but his interpretation took a somewhat poetic and mystical turn, which may have rendered the Prussian Kant suspect to more empirically minded Britons. Even in Germany, however, Kant suffered indifference and neglect during the middle of the nineteenth century, until fortune – in the person of Wilhelm Dilthey and others – turned a kindlier eye upon him and persuaded the Berlin Academy to publish a standard edition of his works. As for British thought, it was not until Scottish theological students, who spent their fourth year of studies in Germany, "discovered" Kant and Hegel that these thinkers were brought into serious consideration in the English-speaking world. We have only to think of the great Scottish commentators to appreciate the eventual influence of Kant's thought,[1] an interest more recently taken up by English philosophers, such as Strawson and others. So much, then, for his explosive

1 James Hutcheson Stirling had published a book on Kant prior to his more famous book on Hegel (*The Secret of Hegel* [London, 1865]). The list of distinguished commentators and translators includes N. Kemp Smith and H.J. Paton.

presence on the thought scene. For our purposes, however, I will imitate the nineteenth-century cry of the resurgent study of the philosopher himself: *Back to Kant!*[2]

For, having sketched *how* this bleaching out of the integrity of things happened, we need to ask also *why* it did. And that is not easy to answer, since it involves a good many influences besides those of philosophy. Marx to the contrary, philosophers are not meant to change the world immediately and directly; they are meant to understand it. Sometimes their interpretations have effect, especially when, as with Kant, there is a "fit" between the philosopher's thought and the prevailing winds of cultural change. Indeed, modern thought is the reflection of those winds, principal of which is the increased sense of individual freedom. And it is here that we must look to find the positive insight that has both impelled the modern process and justified it. As already indicated, the canonical expression of this insight and urge (*conatus*)[3] is to be found in the philosophy of Kant. In his first *Critique* he sealed the modern fate of physical things by reducing them to phenomena, thus fulfilling the possibilites latent within the Cartesian turn and also clearing the ground for a new sense of freedom, which he was to develop in the latter part of the first *Critique* and more extensively in the second and third *Critiques*.

I have already pointed out the inversion of thought and being which was initiated by Descartes in the *Discourse on Method* and consummated by Kant in the preface to the second edition of the *Critique of Pure Reason*: I will call this the *first inversion*, since a more radical one is already on the horizon in Kant's thought. In the previous chapter I indicated how he positioned nature in the witness box, compelling it to answer questions drawn up after a plan of Reason's own demands. Kant then drew the subsequent enquiry to its completion. In the penultimate chapter of the first *Critique*, entitled "The Architectonic of Pure Reason," he sketched the profile of philosophy under the concept of totality [*Totalitätsbegriff*]. Philosophy could take its proper form only as an architectonic system, a totality of meaning that satisfied the "essential needs of reason." As mentioned, Kant framed these essential needs in terms of three questions. The first was "What *can* I know?"; to which he had already replied, "Only appearances, not things in themselves." The second

2 I have distilled much of the foregoing from contemporary and later biographies. See my article "Immanuel Kant (1724–1804): Philosopher of Reason," in *German-Canadian Year Book* (Toronto, 1975), vol. 2, 253–64.

3 The earlier sense of *conatus* is tempered in Kant by a new sense of critical rationality, but it is still operative in the non-cognitive character of practical reason which is all but identified with the will.

was "What *ought* I to do?"; in answer to that question he had drawn the distinction in the first *Critique* between the determinism operative in nature (mechanistic causality) and the necessity operative in freedom (moral obligation). The necessity invoked in moral obligation respected freedom inasmuch as, while the determinisms of nature unavoidably compelled, the command of duty obliged but could be set aside. Kant was to reply more fully in the second *Critique*: "Do your duty in accordance with the demands of practical reason." And finally, Reason put the third question, "What *may* I hope?"; to which Kant was to reply with what has sometimes been called his fourth *Critique*, namely, the treatise *Religion within the Bounds of Reason*. In it, while consistently denying the possibility of any theoretical cognition about the ideas of soul and God, he found rational moral grounds, that is, practical reasons, for rational faith, for postulating the immortality of the soul and the existence of God as guarantor of the union of virtue with happiness.

To appreciate better what is at stake in his thought, it helps to recall the context in which Kant formulated his critical idealism, which had reduced the sphere of theoretical knowledge (cognition: *Erkenntnis*) to phenomena. Kant took up the cudgels of criticism in order to rescue Reason. If we ask, From what? we are told that the old metaphysics was guilty of *dogmatism*. It pretended to a knowledge of things as they really are and not simply as they appear to us. To rectify this presumption, Kant inverted the orders of thought and being (already in principle inverted by Descartes); in Kant's own terms, he effected the inversion of the a priori (the categories of understanding) and the a posteriori (the data of experience). He likened the inversion in the order of thought to the Copernican revolution in the science of astronomy. For the new astronomy had posited the sun as the centre of its field of investigation. And, just as in astronomy the new centre was the sun with its light, so in epistemology the new centre was the light of Reason,[4] once it had become critically aware of both its power and its limits.

Kant understood his critical turn to be the liberation of Reason from its self-imposed bondage.[5] For criticism set Reason free from what he took to be the *dogmatism* of the older traditional metaphysics and its claim to know things as they are, a claim that he encountered in the ambivalent form given to it by the eigheenth-century philosopher Christian Wolff. Kant's critical turn was taken in order to set Reason upon the sure path of science, the royal road to justified knowledge; but even more, if

4 Cf. Descartes' *lumen naturale* in the *Meditations*.
5 Cf. his essay on the autonomy of "public" reason: *What Is Enlightenment?*

less obviously, the critical turn set Reason on the path to its own self-understanding. It was to know itself in terms of itself, and not as a special kind of being in the midst of other beings.

We have seen the loss of ontological weight brought about by the early modern sense of objectivity which made the transition to phenomena all the easier. But we need to stop here and ask why the ontological weight of things had come to be felt as dogmatism. Why had such an understanding of things pressed like a dead weight upon the power and the possibilities of Reason? No doubt, the metaphysical sense of things escaped Reason in its self-appointed authoritative status as judge advocate; for, as we have seen, unlike phenomena, *their* centre (the metaphysical centre of things considered as being) was elsewhere than in the human subject. Indeed, at first glance, Kant's quarrel with traditional metaphysics seems to be primarily a quarrel about the status of things. To which he replies that the thing in itself as it is (*Ding an sich*) is unknowable; what is knowable is only the thing as it appears to us. But we must persist: What is it, then, that renders things-as-they-are opaque to cognition? What condemned to baseless dogmatism the assertion that we know things? I have suggested that it is the "thickness" of things, their relative independence of the knowing powers, their original integrity that withstands the attempt of knowledge to suborn them, that refuses to surrender their original status as creatures which find their centre in a transcendent and creative Source.

But this is not an entirely adequate answer. For we can persist in asking: *Why* has modern thought *needed* to bleach out things into objects determined by method and then into appearances confined by criticism to the putative limits of human cognition? Why in Kant's eyes does the older stance condemn it to dogmatism? There can be no doubt that the ontological weight of things was felt to be an imposition upon the new sense of the character, scope, and limits of Reason. It is not, therefore, so much primarily a question of the nature and status of things as it is more radically a question of the nature and scope of thought. It is confirmation of Kant's importance that the issue of the nature of rationality is still with us.[6] It was not that critical reason could wrench itself arbitrarily from the context of objectivity, but rather that, given its pre-eminence,

6 And still present at a most fundamental level which challenges the very continuance of philosophy itself. See the discussion by Karl Otto, Jürgen Habermas, Paul Ricoeur, Jean-François Lyotard, and others in K. Baynes *et al.*, ed., *After Philosophy: End or Transformation?* (Cambridge, Mass.: MIT 1987).

Reason had to find new sources of order *within* itself.[7] It found those resources in the famous Kantian a priori categories and their even more important a priori application in the Schematism and the Principles of the first *Critique.* In so doing, the critical turn further advanced the Cartesian withdrawal from things; it did this in order to provide objects with a new context, more amenable to Reason's own self-discovery. In the wake of Kant, later thinkers were to locate those resources within consciousness itself: in moral duty and ethical earnestness with Fichte, in transcendental artistic creativity with the early Schelling and many of the Romantics, and in the dialectical self-determination of Absolute Spirit with Hegel. No doubt, it was easier to subvert phenomena than things; and no doubt, too, the transition from things to objects paved the way for their reduction to appearances. The lightness of things in the critical idealism of Kant came about by lifting the weight attributed to them by the old metaphysics, a weight that had already been all but lost in the medium of modern objectivity.

That weight was taken from the scales because it no longer provided the measure for a Reason armed with self-criticism. Nor was the weight restored by the post-Kantian rejection of the doctrine of the unknowable *Ding-an-sich,* neither by the Absolute Idealists, Schelling and Hegel, nor much later by the Neo-Kantians, such as Hermann Cohen. Instead, any attempt to restore the traditional metaphysical sense of things was still perceived to be a dogmatic weight – an unreasonable weight that brought Reason into an unwarranted dependency. The autonomy of Reason triumphed over its alleged heteronomy to things. The lightness of phenomena replaced the sturdiness of things in Kant's critical idealism in the interest of defending Reason's own freedom, even though Kant attributed a purely rational character to that freedom. Later thinkers, such as Kierkegaard and Nietzche, but also, in his own way, Marx, would do otherwise.

Indeed, the lightness of phenomena persists in Kant's immediate successors even after they have withdrawn the restriction of knowledge to appearances. For with the abandonment of the untenable notion of the thing-in-itself, critical reason sealed its own horizon, a horizon left open to the insertion of experienced content in the constitution of empirical objectivity. Among Kant's more independent successors, Schelling and

7 This is in tune with the growing sense of the autonomy of reason which was developing throughout the seventeenth and eighteenth centuries. In the *Education of the Human Race* (Leipzig, 1855), vol. 2, 348–54, Lessing already finds within Reason alone the truths necessary for human fulfillment.

Hegel, Reason in the form of the Absolute expanded to include all that presents itself to consciousness. Notwithstanding, the critical attitude was still maintained by Kant's successors. Previously, the older metaphysics of the Aristotelian kind had sought to confirm the reality of its knowledge by a noetic encounter with things. Now, in Schelling and Hegel, the new critical attitude confirmed the scope of thought by the power of inclusion, that is, by expanding the horizon of thought's concern and manifesting its ability to interpret such fields as history, art, and religion with new power.[8] But, even though the *unknowability of the Ding-an-sich* was rejected, the weight with which metaphysical things had previously seemed to press upon consciousness was not thereby restored.[9]

This is because the quarrel, after all, was not so much about the status of things as about the capacities of reason; not a question about the constitution of things, but one about the nature of rationality.[10] Admittedly, insofar as things had been converted into objects, they were subject-determined and subject-dependent; that is the trajectory of classical modern philosophy. But, strictly speaking, dogmatism is not an attribute of things; it is rather an attitude of reason, a conception of rationality. So that the solution called for a redefinition of reason. Against the dogmatism of things, Kant posited "the critical attitude" of Pure Reason.

He was shocked when the first reviews of his *Critique of Pure Reason* tended to lump his thought together with the dogmatic idealism of Bishop Berkeley, and he preferred to call his own philosophy "critical or transcendental idealism."[11] The critical attitude relinquishes all claims on behalf of reason to know things as they really are; but the rejection arises not primarily from the shock of an encounter with things too "thick" and full-bodied for reason to digest – their day was long past. Instead, the rejection derives from reason's own self-criticism, once it has

8 It was the new (unlimited) scope of reason that inspired Hegel's criticism of Kant in *Glauben und Wissen* and the *Differenzschrift* and not any restoration of the metaphyics of things (*res*).

9 Milan Kundera catches a literary version of this loss of weight in his novel *The Unbearable Lightness of Being* (1984, repr. Harper Perennial 1991).

10 There can be no doubt that such a question has been seen as part of the Kantian heritage. Here again, see the many versions of rationality in Theodore Geraets, ed., *Rationalité aujourdhui/Rationality Today* (Ottawa: University of Ottawa Press 1979).

11 See the first *Critique* at B274: "Der dogmatische Idealismus ist unvermeidlich, wenn man den Raum als Eigenschaft, die den Dingen an sich selbst zukommen soll, ansieht; denn da ist er mit allem, dem er zur Bedingung dient, ein Unding." He then pronounces his own "transcendental idealism" free of such difficulty. See also A369 and the footnote at B xxxix–xli.

assumed primacy over things which have been reduced to objects and further to appearances.

Still, that is a negative way of putting the issue. The positive motivation was to maintain the primacy of the human subject in its double role. For, as already mentioned in the previous chapter, Reason faced the object over against it (in its role as empirical subject), while at the same time (in its role as transcendental subject) it laid down the terms for what was to count as acceptable in regard to the object. In this valorization, the Kantian subject laid no claim to the creation of things; indeed, it bears repeating that creation (hence things as creatures) became a dead issue for philosophical reason. Kant's first *Critique* is not to be understood as the *construction* of a phenomenal world, as though Reason were a demi-god; rather, it is to be understood as giving noetic validity and authority to the theoretical project of Reason, once reason is freed of its metaphysical dogmatism through the adoption of the critical attitude.[12]

To appreciate the positive motivation for the critical turn, then, and before turning to the third *Critique* in which Kant thought he had resolved the outstanding issues of his philosophy, we should glance briefly at Kant's popular essay *What Is Enlightenment?* In it, he sums up, with characteristic perspicacity, the essential profile of the Enlightenment ideal of *freedom.* This permits us to trace the trajectory of Kant's philosophy in three steps: first, the charge against dogmatism; second, its resolution in criticism; and third, its culmination in freedom.

In the *Essay* Kant tells us that freedom can be attained only if we have the courage to break away from all subservient tutelage: *sapere aude!* It is as though Kant counsels us: Do not begin with the problematic idealism of Descartes ("I think, therefore I am") for that still associates thought with some version of being (I am; *res cogitans*); begin, rather, with the critical project ("Dare to think freely!"). Uncritical dependence is proper enough for children, he concedes, but it is servile in an adult. Of course, obedience takes many forms; some are entered into freely, and may even be legitimate, insofar as they contribute to the good order of society. Thus, if he is to hold his post within the church, the ordained minister is required to preach according to the rule of his denomination, that is, in conformity with the particular form of the Creed laid

12 See my essay "The Idealism of the German Romantics," in M. Baur and D. Dahlstrom, ed., *The Emergence of German Idealism* (Studies in Philosophy and the History of Philosophy, vol. 34) (Washington, D.C.: Catholic University of America 1999), 176–97, in particular 185n.21.

down by his sect. So, too, a soldier is obliged to obey the commands given to him in battle or on parade, and a bureaucrat needs to follow the procedures laid down by the government he has sworn to serve. All of this belongs to their official positions, which Kant refers to as belonging to the "private" sphere. The sphere is private because, insofar as the person has accepted certain restrictions as to what he can say or do in discharging certain functions, he is, to that degree and while he is discharging them, deprived (cf. *privatus*) of full participation in the public life of free thought.

In the "public" sphere, on the other hand, that is, in the sphere of educated persons, freedom comes into its own. In the republic of free spirits (to use a term favoured by Leibniz), the minister when in his study and not in the pulpit, the soldier when in mufti and not in uniform, the bureaucrat when at leisure and not in his office, not only may but ought to speak out freely. The minister is free – nay! obligated, if he dares to think bravely – to publish his views on the Creed and the Scriptures, even when they contradict the beliefs of his denomination; the soldier is free to speak and write critically of the military, even though his views may conflict with military strategy; and the bureaucrat is free to disagree with his government's policy. Confident of the progressive nature of rational freedom, Kant insists that there is only one requirement: that insofar as they hold official (that is, "private") positions in society, each must obey the relevant authority when he is acting in virtue of his official position: the minister must obey the conditions laid down by the church (or be defrocked), the soldier must execute the commands of the army (or be cashiered), and the bureaucrat must follow the policies of the government without criticism (or be dismissed); otherwise, Kant argues, civil order would be destroyed. To which he adds, more generally, that the citizen must observe the laws.

Having all but equated the will with reason in its practical mode, Kant was not troubled by the divorce of theoretical thought from practice. And so he did not think that the eulogy to individual freedom in the public sphere would introduce anarchy into society, for he insisted that even in the public sphere each is obligated by the internal demands of reason, which he held to be rather more obvious and compelling than many of us do, at least since Freud has made us wary of rational explanations which may harbour unstated wilfulness (cf. "rationalization," ideology). The value that prompts the Kantian commitment to free expression in the public sphere is freedom understood as *individual autonomy*, practical reason's own self-legislation.

We may recognize a more positive aspect, however, in Kant's breaking away in matters of freedom from the determinisms of modern cognition theory (*Erkenntnis*), to "make room" for practical knowing in the form of a rational "faith." In so doing, Kant has implicitly expanded the scope of a certain sort of "knowing" (*Wissen*) beyond the restriction to modern cognition, though this mode of "knowing" did not permit him to make assertions concerning the nature and existence of things. It is, therefore, still far from an endorsement of the classical notion of *theôria.* We shall return to this point as we reflect upon what I have called the "new freedom."

The first inversion of thought over being was made easier by the earlier methodical, epistemological idealism which denuded Nature of things and reduced the community of beings to a system of objects and, eventually, to an architectonic system of phenomena. The first Cartesian inversion – that of cognitive thought over being – prepared the way for a second Kantian inversion: that of freedom over the determinisms of Nature. We have seen that the two-stage reduction from things to objects and from objects to phenomena cleared the way for an emergent subjectivity and its claims, a subjectivity no longer merely set over against objectivity but superior to it.

The decisive passage is to be found in Kant's analysis of the dynamically sublime [*das Erhabene*] in the third *Critique.* There he recounts the experience by which we encounter the sheer forces of Nature, not directly, however, as the cause of terror and physical injury, for that would subject us to the determinisms of Nature. The experience of the dynamically sublime must take place in such a way that the encounter with the sheer physical forces of Nature occurs from a place of physical security. (Imagine yourself at Niagara Falls on the *Maid of the Mist,* wet with spray at the base of the thundering Falls.) It is this combination of awesome natural power and human safety that gives rise to the awareness that, after all, rage as Nature might, we are superior to it; for in our practical subjectivity we are free of the determinisms of Nature. We will readily recognize that the mighty forces of Nature are fearful, and produce in us a feeling of awe, but what Kant makes of this experience is worth reflecting upon, worth quoting at length:

> Bold, overhanging, and as it were, threatening, rocks; thunderclouds piled up in the vault of heaven, borne along with lightning flashes and thunder peals; volcanoes in all violence of destruction; hurricances with their track of devastation; the boundless ocean in a state of rebellion and upheaval [*Empörung*]; the lofty waterfall of a mighty river, and such like; these make our power of resistance of

trifling moment in comparison with their might. But the sight of them becomes the more attractive, the more fearful it is, provided only that our own position is secure; and we readily call these objects sublime, because they raise the forces of the soul [*Seelenstärke*] above its usual measure [*gewöhnliches Mittelmass*], and discover in us a power of resistance [*ein Vermögen zu widerstehen*] of a quite different kind, which gives us courage to be able to measure ourselves against the seeming omnipotence of nature ... [Reflecting upon this experience of the overwhelming immensity of nature, Kant remarks that we have found in it "our own limitation"], although at the same time in our rational faculty we have found a different, non-sensuous standard, which has that infinity itself under it as unity [*als Einheit*], and in comparison with which everything in nature is small. Thus in our mind [*Gemüthe*] we have found a superiority over [*Überlegenheit über*] nature even in its immeasurability [*Unermesslichkeit*]. And so also, the irresistibility of its might [*Unwiderstehlichkeit ihrer Macht*], while making us recognise our own physical impotence, considered as beings of nature [*Naturwesen*], discloses to us a faculty of judging independently of, and a superiority over, nature.[13]

Kant's close student Friedrich Schiller, poet, dramatist, essayist, and educator, developed the theme of moral superiority in two essays on the sublime.[14] "We call an object sublime if, whenever the object is presented or represented, our sensuous nature feels its limits, but our rational nature feels its superiority, its freedom from limits. Thus, we come up short against a sublime object *physically*, but we elevate ourselves above it *morally*, namely through ideas." Indeed, "the will is what distinguishes the human race, and reason itself is nothing but the will's everlasting rule." And finally:

Human freedom would quickly be at an end, if a human being were capable only of physical culture. However, he is supposed to be a human being without exception [i.e., absolutely]; thus, in no case is he supposed to suffer or undergo something *against* his will. If he can no longer oppose physical forces with a corresponding physical force, then nothing else remains for him to do to avoid suffering violence than *to do completely away with a relation* so deleterious to him and

13 The above translation has mixed those of J.H. Bernard and J.C. Meredith, while slightly modifying both. For the German, see *Kritik der Urtheilskraft*, I, ii, B, no. 28; Akademie Textausgabe, vol. 5 (Berlin: Walter Gruyter 1968), 261–2.

14 *Vom Erhabenen* ("On the Sublime") and *Über das Erhabene* ("Concerning the Sublime"). English translation in Walter Hinderer and Daniel Dahlstrom, ed., *Friedrich Schiller: Essays* vol. 17 of *The German Library* series (New York: Continuum 1993), 22, 70.

to *destroy conceptually* a brute force that he in fact must endure. However, to destroy a force conceptually means nothing other than to submit to it voluntarily. The culture that renders him adept at this is called "the moral culture."[15]

This understanding of freedom is fundamental and, as Kant touches upon it, infinite in its own order.[16] It is not the metaphysical understanding of freedom, which sees freedom exercised within the community of beings.[17] Kant's ethical thought is often described as *deontic*,[18] in contrast to a teleological ethics. While this characterization is not incorrect, it does not quite catch the gist of the new sense of freedom. Those of us who are familiar with the meaning of liberty in the English and French style may be bemused when we hear German intellectuals refer to their own tradition as one of freedom. This is understandable, given the events of the last one hundred and fifty years along with the caricature associated with that calamitous history. But, if we can get past this barrier, it may be of profit to trace out the difference in the different conceptions of freedom. For, in the tradition of German idealism, what is meant by freedom encompasses a whole sphere, a totality (Schiller's "without exception") that is not restricted to freedom of choice among

15 This bears some anticipatory affinity with Nietzsche's empowerment of the will through the teaching of the eternal return, which intended to accept all the past as the effect of one's having willed it. In Nietzsche, the primacy of reason becomes the primacy of the will, so that Nietzsche completes the course of *conatus*. The decisive role and status accorded to him by Heidegger and postmodernists suggests, however, that the attraction of *conatus* still exercises its power over a significant group of philosophers. Once again, *conatus* differs from the medieval Aristotelian *appetitus* in that the latter is situated within a context of natures possessing determinate ends. Jacques Maritain's retrieval of *inclinatio* in St Thomas may be seen as an attempt to accommodate something of the *élan* and impetus of *conatus* within the horizon of a traditional metaphysics of being.

16 Reminiscent of Descartes's conception of the infinitude of the will, Kant's use of the word "infinity" is also reminiscent of Spinoza's distinction of that which is infinite "after its own kind." (*Ethics* I, definition VI.) Writing of God, Spinoza asserts: "I say absolutely infinite, not infinite after its kind; for, of a thing infinite only after its kind [as are extension and thought], infinite attributes may be denied." (Cf. definition II: "finite after its kind.") We see here the roots of the contemporary endowment of the finite with a certain absolute character, while at the same time denying to it any claim to unqualified infinitude.

17 For a detailed insight into the conception of freedom in Kant, see the excellent study by Richard Velkley, *Freedom and the End of Reason: On the Moral Foundation of Kant's Critical Philosophy* (Chicago: University of Chicago Press 1989).

18 Jeremy Bentham's *Deontology* (published in 1834 posthumously and partly a collection of notes) is based upon a utilitarian rather than a transcendental philosophy, but his concept of "fictitious entities" calls into play the free activity of the imagination and is directed against a teleological ethics.

finite alternatives. Such an understanding of freedom differs also from the traditional metaphysical notion of freedom as free will *(liberum arbitrium)*; for that is a faculty of deliberation and choice, and is the progenitor of the English and French understanding.[19] There is instead an element of creative spontaneity in this new sense of freedom, a spontaneity not entirely divorced from the earlier *conatus* and already laying the ground for the later empowerment of creative imagination.

Kant insists that the superiority of freedom is of "a quite different kind" [*von ganz andrer Art*] from the mighty determinisms of Nature. Admittedly, Kant himself interpreted this freedom rather narrowly in terms of morality, as did Fichte, but his remarks on the role of the imagination, like those also of Fichte, suggest that Kant's remarks can bear a somewhat broader range of reference. This is because what I have called the new freedom is of a quite other kind, not only from the mighty determinisms of Nature, but also from the conventional view of freedom as the capacity to choose among alternatives.

In the two essays on the sublime that breathe with the influence of Kant, Friedrich Schiller gives full scope to the creative role of the imagination. To be sure, the new freedom is not the freedom of a Creator of being *ex nihilo*; but neither is it in principle simply a moral freedom in any narrow sense. It hovers in between, achieving less than *creatio ex nihilo* but more than epistemological validity or moral autonomy. It is not accidental that Schiller highlights the medium of play, to which belongs a distinctive form of freedom. The new freedom elevates the human subject in the whole of his being. This "more" (than epistemological or moral) became evident when Schelling and Hegel expanded the new power through the notion of Absolute Spirit with its dynamism of absolute self-determination, thereby recovering fields beyond those of epistemic and moral values, including the fields of history, aesthetics, and religion, in a word the whole of human concern.[20]

19 More precisely, there are three different conceptions of freedom: the broader metaphysical sense, which places the deliberative factor of choice within a primordial teleological ordination to an ultimate Good; the narrower and more psychological Anglo-French modern restriction to choice; and the more fundamental and broader ontological sense found in the German tradition.

20 This sense of freedom is prepared for by Kant's distinction between the reflective and the determinant judgments. The latter are bound by necessity to the categories and function in the Schematism of the first *Critique*; while the former are free of the concept. "The reflective judgment, is more free from external controls and allows the imagination to create its own ideas for organizing experience as a formally purposive system." See Rudolph A. Makreel, *Imagination and Interpretation in Kant: The Hermeneutical Import of the Critique of Judgment* (Chicago: University of Chicago Press 1990), 3.

Hegel often remarked upon the need to wed the ontology of the ancients with the subjectivity of the moderns, while expanding the latter to its absolute measure. And, indeed, the infinite subjectivity of Absolute Spirit moves with the new freedom. For Hegel, infinite subjectivity is not only the locus of cognition but also the preserve of freedom. Absolute Spirit is no longer tied to the introspective inwardness of the Cartesian psyche, but neither does it possess the realistic interiority of metaphysical principles; it displays itself instead in the stages of its own self-determination.[21]

Such self-determination aims at more than the epistemological goal of a system of phenomena schematized according to a priori categories and ordered according to empirically verifiable laws (Kant). The new sense of the primacy of the subject, now become infinite subjectivity (Hegel), releases a new sense, not of creation, but of *creativity* based upon the superiority of the subject in its new-found freedom. Despite its flaws (its inability to overcome the presuppositions of modern idealism and the primacy of subjectivity), this is a step towards recovering an ontological (in contrast to a merely deliberative) sense of freedom.

To that degree, the post-Kantian philosophies project an advance upon both the moral sense upheld by Kant, Fichte, and, to some extent, Schiller and the conventional Anglo-French understanding of freedom as the power of choice. One might even say that they bring forward a new element at best only implicit in the traditional metaphysical *liberum arbitrium.* I say "at best only implicit," because there is among medieval thinkers a deeper sense of freedom as the primordial ordination of the creature to the good of itself and community, an ordination that lies ontologically prior to the exercise of freedom through choice. It is here that I see the possibility of acknowledging the new and more powerful appreciation of freedom, once it is re-implanted in the ontological context of a traditional metaphysics.

There can be no doubt, too, that, despite their radical differences, there is a certain rapprochement between these speculative philosophies (of Schelling and Hegel) and the metaphysics of being.[22] Indeed, these philosophers have striven to recover certain insights associated

21 In the *Science of Logic,* Hegel overcomes (*aufhebt*) the distinction of inner and outer, though in favour ultimately of the self-determination of absolute subjectivity. It is for this reason that – with a touch of irony, if not of paradox – one can say of this profound thinker that there is strictly no depth in his thought. All is delivered over to the manifestation of Spirit's self-expression.

22 The term "speculative" here bears a technical meaning. In fashioning a post-Kantian ontology, the term designates the attempt to go beyond Kant's critical idealism with its restriction to phenomena.

with ontology and to resituate them within an expanded modern context. Hegel sought to reconcile what he called the ancient objectivity of being with the modern penchant for subjectivity. His emphasis on subjectivity, however, committed him to a metaphysical idealism. My present intention is just the reverse, since it attempts to acknowledge the value of the modern experience, with its emphasis upon subjectivity, while incorporating its insight into freedom within the horizon of a metaphysics of being. These speculative philosophies are by no means uncontested in modern thought. On the contrary, it is clear that, except for the modern transcendental philosophies, there is in the current approach an implicit – and often explicit – tendency to appeal to materialistic explanations; in a word, to read reality "from below." By invoking the notion of Spirit (*Geist*), the speculative philosophies of Schelling and Hegel are able to take non-reductionist account of the so-called "works of the spirit," and particularly of culture, art, and religion. Moreover, the advantage of reinstating the new freedom in the context of the metaphysics of being is that a more adequate account of the realistic thrust of knowledge (hence of a renewed sense of realism in modern science) is possible. For the concept of Spirit enables these philosophers to enlarge their vision and incorporate dimensions of experience that are accounted for by materialistic explanations only in a reductive, minimal, and artificial way. In a word, these speculative philosophies read reality "from above."

But, as they currently are, they remain too much within the orbit of the logic of modernity insofar as they still give primacy to the human subject as providing the overriding model for their interpretation of reality. This results in the ambiguity in Hegel's account of freedom and the minimalizing tendencies in his treatment of transcendence.[23] The advantage of the metaphysics of being is that it provides an expansive enough horizon to accommodate both human subjectivity and natural things in their integrity and not simply as moments of the absolute System. Indeed, the metaphysical notion of thing (*res*) as equivalent with being (*ens*) is capacious enough to "fit" both persons and things. For, while traditional metaphysics considers all things in the emphatic sense

23 See especially the latter part of the Berlin *Lectures on the Philosophy of Religion*, vol. 3, Peter Hodgson, ed., *The Consummate Religion* (Berkeley: University of California Press 1985), particularly his treatment of creation, immortality, the resurrection of the person of Christ, and the community of faith. For example, instead of the frank attribution of gratuity to the act of creation (as in *creatio ex nihilo*), Hegel struggles to avoid a certain necessary emanationism in his treatment of creation, without notable success.

to be subjects (that is, subjects of being), the concept of subject as the central core of each thing embraces other aspects of reality (such as accidents). The modern concept of subject, on the other hand, confined as it is to human thought, sensibility, or feeling – that is, to Descartes-Kant, Hume, and Rousseau, respectively – is too restricted to provide an ample enough horizon for the accommodation of all of reality. It is inescapably reductive. It has to tailor reality to its own compass and measure. The failure to recognize a genuine transcendence beyond that of human subjectivity (and even of absolute subjectivity, which is patterned after the human) can be remedied only by moving beyond it to the broader horizon of being. Only such a move can do justice to transcendence philosophically by letting the otherness of things (*aliquid*)[24] come into play in a radical way; and only through the recognition of a radical transcendence can freedom be truly free.

Let me try once more to delineate the sense in which the "new freedom" is both "free" and "new," and to reflect more closely upon the relation between the metaphysics of things and the new sense of freedom. There are obvious differences between the understanding of freedom in the metaphysics of being and the understanding of freedom in modern thought, particularly in its most radical expression, namely, in the transcendental philosophy of Kant and the speculative philosophies of his successors.

But, if the differences are clear, less obvious are the affinities and convergences. Indeed, the new freedom represents both a challenge and an opportunity for the recovery of things in their integrity. Since each approach aims to be fundamental, we must not expect an easy compromise or synthesis without residue. Nevertheless, if (as I have proposed) the recovery of a "thick" sense of things is imperative not only for their sake but for ours as well, neither can the vigorous and sustained modern experience of freedom be ignored; for it, too, must carry within it some truth about reality. Somewhat in the way in which a religious faith might illuminate an aspect of reality which must then be appropriated by philosophical means, so, too, the modern experience shows forth lights that permit us to take our bearing even as we proceed along another path than the one conventionally taken in modern culture – lights that need to be appropriated by a metaphysics of being. And so we must ask

24 *Aliquid* (something other) is one of the transcendental properties of being and the ground of relation as such. Moreover, it expresses the primordial relationality that is analogically intrinsic to being itself.

whether modern experience points back to resources in metaphysics that call for a further thoughtful development of this cultural deposit.

To begin with the differences, the new freedom is not new in the sense that it has no connections at all with earlier ideas of freedom. Still, it did arise in the modern context and under modern conditions, and the differences are marked by that career. Positively, modern experience moves with the intensification of freedom that is the pre-eminent feature of the modern era. Negatively, such freedom is the motive for the reduction of things to objects and to phenomena. The new freedom is recursive, self-referential, centred in the subject understood as some form of consciousness, which embraces both mind and will. Indeed, it has taken various forms in its modern career: as the Cartesian mind with its minimal liberty of indifference, as the Kantian ego with its non-cognitive freedom as rational faith, as the absolute self-determination of the expanded subjectivity (Absolute Spirit) of Kant's successors, and even as Nietzsche's absolutism of the Will to Power.

The early modern stress on freedom as the exercise of choice is an extension, intensification, and localization of elective freedom. Centred in the individual, it is the hallmark of classical liberalism. In its modern dress, it is not an appetite in Aristotle's sense of a rational desire. For it is not principally and intrinsically a relation to an other as embodying their mutual good, inasmuch as a proper use of human freedom with respect to things brings about both the good of things and of the human being. Rather, the modern sense of freedom is related to itself as to its own pre-eminent good. Such freedom is wholly self-affirming once it has torn loose from its identification with appetite. For it is not simply the freedom to choose among alternatives presented to it by others (heteronomy), but is the freedom to affirm itself through "un-choosing" its past choices (autonomy).[25] To that degree, the new freedom is radically anti-traditional, even to the point of inventing institutions whose primary function is the negative criticism of existing alternatives. Driven by the same logic, popular culture overvalues novelty; its trademark is "New and Improved."

Intensification through *conatus* and localization in the individual is marked by the negativity inherent within the seventeenth-century rejection of final causes, that is, the rejection of the orientation of a thing

25 Such freedom is not locked into its choices. The inherent dynamism of elective freedom pushes it towards the repeated rescue of itself through the renewal of the power to choose. See "Is Liberalism Good Enough?" in R. Bruce Douglass *et al.*, ed., *Liberalism and the Good* (New York: Routledge 1990).

towards an other as towards its own good. We have here again, in the absolution of freedom from everything except itself, an instance of attributing to something finite an infinite colouring, insofar as freedom has been characterized without reference to the end (*finis*). Here we meet again an "infinity after its own kind." It is a general feature of the logic of modernity that it attempts to absorb aspects of positive infinitude into the context of the finite as part of a more general strategy of the reduction of all transcendence to the horizon of immanent human concerns.

Once freedom is "freed" from a teleological relation to the other as its good, it comes to be understood as absolute self-affirmation – whether in accord with Reason or Passion, whether localized in the human individual or the collectivity of the state or expanded into Absolute Spirit. In each of these the logic of self-reference is operative. The seeds of that logic are found in the notion of *conatus*, so prevalent in the early modern period. The forebear of the new sense of freedom is, as just remarked, a *conatus* that is disengaged from an appetitive drive oriented towards natured things capable of satisfying (and, at least for a time, completing, fulfilling, or finalizing) the appetite. When *conatus* follows its inherent path of non-teleological self-affirmation, it becomes *causa sui*, self-moving and self-validating.[26] As we saw in the previous chapter, Bella Abzug formulated the idea precisely in her cry "It does not matter *what* you choose! It only matters *that* you choose!"

Let us return to Kant. And, first, I will remark upon the method in my reflections on Kant. In what follows I do not attempt an historical interpretation of the philosophy of Kant in its completeness, nor do I suggest that Kant ever has or would have taken the notion of freedom so radically as here presented. But I do press Kant in regard to the logic inherent in the central movement of his thought. To do justice to the fullness of Kant's philosophy, one would have to take into account other factors, for the actual philosophy of any great thinker always attempts to accommodate the full range of the various aspects of experience and do justice to them. Nevertheless, in any consistent thinker, there is always a central principle at work and it is this to which I attend here. To take an example: it is not incorrect to focus upon Kant's categorical imperative and the command to duty as essential to Kant's thought, just because it is

26 The absolutism of freedom finds its parallel expression in the physical order among the sciences of motion as such, which take motion (in particular impetus) to be a primitive notion requiring no explanation through reduction to a domain that transcends motion (Aristotle's Unmoved Mover). This parallelism suggests a profound cultural movement in the modern era which finds its expression both in the physical order and in the sphere of freedom.

central. Still, there is more to Kant's ethics than the categorical imperative, as his *Lectures on Ethics and Jurisprudence* show, and a full presentation of his thought would require acknowledgement of these. What justifies concentration upon the central principle, however, is that the logic of which it is the expression subordinates the other elements to its demands. So, too, in what follows. The fact that Kant attends to other factors does not detract from the centrality of his demand for autonomous freedom. And, more generally, it is this logic that I find central to the various versions of what I have called the logic of modernity. That logic will press towards its preferred consequences – especially in shaping popular culture, which tends to disregard nuances and qualifications in favour of simplicity.

It is worth noticing that the charge of dogmatism now reappears in the practical order. You will recall that, for Kant, the weight of things oppressed the cognitive powers in their search for the certitude of scientific cognition; so that Kant confessed that he had to "clip the wings" of knowledge in order to "make room for faith." The weight of otherness, even though only minimally present in phenomena, still pressed too hard upon freedom, which answered not to others but only to itself as pure practical Reason. In the sphere of *praxis*, of course, the charge of dogmatism takes form in relation to freedom. Given that the new freedom is taken to be a self-affirming value, the weight of things now presses upon the very aspiration for freedom.

What becomes the issue in regard to freedom, then, is not the capacity of other things to satisfy an appetite, but the new freedom's own power to vindicate its absolute autonomy. The weight of other things upon freedom is comparable to the weight of other things upon the powers of cognition; and that weight is open on the same grounds to the charge of dogmatism. But what for cognition constitutes dogmatism, for freedom becomes unwarranted dependence or oppression. Dogmatism in the order of freedom is heteronomy. It is this allegedly oppressive weight of the other that, in Kant's essay on the Enlightenment, lies at the root of his sweeping condemnation of all but the most carefully qualified forms of dependency as degrading. It also lies at the base of the rejection of freedom as a movement of appetite. The autonomy of freedom eschews what, in this logic, must be taken to be heteronomy, unwarranted dependence upon another.

The new freedom, therefore, is no longer an appetite for the other as embodying its good, but the affirmation of itself as its own good. Such freedom thus becomes a self-sustaining mode of life (Schiller's "moral culture"), which envelops the subject in its totality (Schiller's "without exception"). Only the logic inherent in such a conative freedom can account for the remarkable way in which the overwhelming presence of the forces of nature is passed over in order to affirm the *total* superiority of the subject in the face of those forces. Such an elevation of the subject changes nothing physically, while the exercise of volition alone establishes the absolute superiority of the subject over nature.

No doubt, there is something noble, if not quixotic, about such an attitude. But such a disregard is possible only insofar as there is a broad "ditch" separating the volitional from the cognitive powers of the human subject. In Kant, the divorce of man from things has reaffirmed a divorce within man himself – a divorce already wrought by the Cartesian dualism of mind and body, of thought and extension. It is on the basis of this anthropological dualism that Kant and Schiller can speak of the "superiority" of the free subject. The radical understanding of such freedom receives its buoyant expression in Nietzsche's Will to Power, and above all in the teaching of the Eternal Recurrence of the Same, by which the will reclaims *as its own work* all that is past and all that will come through the same "gateway" again and again.[27] After the "masters of suspicion," in particular Freud, and after the horrors of this past century, the new freedom receives less sanguine appreciation from postmodernists who are sensitive to the fact that all is not so well as it might be. Once again, the attitude of our higher culture tends to resemble the century of the Black Death more than the Century of Lights (*le siècle des lumières)* and more than the brilliance of the thirteenth century with its high metaphysics. Indeed, a chorus of voices proclaims that the death of God has been followed by the death of man (by which is meant modern humanism).[28] But is it possible that the death of both God and man have followed upon the death of things?

27 *Thus Spake Zarathustra* II: "On Redemption": "To redeem those who lived in the past and to recreate all 'it was' into a 'thus I willed it' – that alone should I call redemption. Will – that is the name of the liberator and joy-bringer ..." At first, Zarathustra is frustrated because "the will itself is still a prisoner" of the past ("it was"). "This, indeed, is what *revenge* is: the will's ill-will against time and its 'it was' ... This, this is what is eternal in the punishment called existence, that existence must eternally become deed and guilt again ... The will is a creator. All 'it was' is a fragment, a riddle, a dreadful accident – until the creative will says to it, 'But thus I willed it.' Until the creative will says to it, 'but thus I will it; thus shall I will it.'" In part III/2 ("On the Vision and the Riddle"), Zarathustra overcomes his nausea and finds joy in a violent act of the will. (Trans. by W. Kaufmann, *The Portable Nietzsche* [New York: Viking 1958], 251–2, 269–72.)

28 Robert de Man, Jacques Derrida, and Michel Foucault, among others, have expressed this view in a variety of ways.

Yet, if the intensification and expansion of freedom offers a challenge to a more traditional metaphysics, it also offers an opportunity for second thoughts. More specifically, the catalyst of the new freedom operative within much of modern experience offers metaphysics an opportunity for a better realization of its own resources. Once the modern divorce of man from nature and the consequent reduction of things is suspected of not being inevitable, the logic of that divorce opens up to critical reflection. This, of course, has been the theme of these reflections. Once the "thick" sense of things has been recovered along with their integrity and relative independence, possibilities present themselves for drawing from the new freedom an understanding that frees freedom from a too close identification with the liberty of choice. Such a catalyst enables us to see within the metaphysics of being indications of a more pervasive and deeper sense of freedom. This, for a traditional metaphysics of things, is the "cash value" of the modern experience. That experience offers a new regard for the intensification and expansion of freedom. And this emphasis cries out to be incorporated within the horizon of the metaphysics of being; indeed, it must be, if being is to vindicate its centuries-long claim to be the comprehensive and all-inclusive horizon of thought and reality. By its own lights, all historical change must be part of the history of being, which includes the new freedom.

We need to ask, though, whether there are indications of this freedom at the heart of things? and whether such freedom must be purchased by the deprivation of the "thick" sense of things? We might start, however surprisingly, with Aristotle's notion of the *voluntary*. The voluntary, he tells us, is a spontaneous movement from within sentient things. In men it undergirds the power of choice. But it is also operative in animals, where liberty of choice is not present. For, while recognizing the *voluntarium* as specific to sentient things, the notion of spontaneity can be extended in a variety of ways to all things: to trees, which literally "reach" out to nutrients, and even to rocks, which enter into active chemical interactions with other things. *Conatus* in its modern version is the absolutism of the voluntary, not by extension (since it is restricted to human willing) but by intension, since, despite its rejection of teleology, it retains the character of intrinsic spontaneity, raising it to the primacy of a first principle. That is why Spinoza and his latter-day confrère Nietzsche could celebrate *conatus* while denying liberty of choice.[29]

29 Upon reading Spinoza, Nietzsche marvelled that he had found a soulmate, that his *Einsamkeit* had become a *Zweisamkeit.* (To Overbeck, 30 July 1881; *The Portable Nietzsche*, 92).

The metaphysics of being is not entirely without a concept that bears affinity with such a *conatus*. In metaphysics, of course, it takes a teleological form. For, insofar as things possess natures endowed with finality, there is present within them a fundamental orientation towards the good, as that which completes or perfects them in some way, as water is good for plants, meat for carnivores, and the *summum bonum* for persons; for the first two, being physical: good in measure; for the last, being spiritual: good without reserve. Moreover, this orientation lies prior to and deeper than any deliberation or choice on their part. It is part of their endowment as creatures.

Thus, given the interiority and depth within the metaphysical constitution of things, what emerges as *conatus* in the modern period is already prefigured in that orientation towards the absolute Good that is part of the constitutive relation with which every creature is endowed as its birthright. And this is true not only of rational creatures who possess deliberative liberty in the exercise of choice, and who by an irrational exercise of choice may frustrate that orientation, but also of all things, whose primordial orientation is to the ordered good of the universe. Here we have a comprehensive teleological dynamism more fundamental than choice. And here, too, we have a restatement of the Greek sense of cosmos, of things moved by a basic and universal ordination to the good of the whole. Yet this teleological dynamism shares some features with a *non-teleological conatus* in that both are intrinsic and spontaneous. The new freedom, then, is the blossoming of a new sense, a deepening of an experience of the dynamism at the root of all things.

Symptoms of this deeper freedom are resident also in the immateriality within each thing. In its expansiveness, each thing "escapes" *in a certain way* from the confinement of the isolated individual which it is. Such immateriality is distinctive of form. I have already mentioned a certain expansive quality in form. On the one hand, the determinism of the modern conception of nature gravitates towards matter as towards a principle of locality and partition. On the other, form is by its very nature an expansive principle moving towards community, for it is unable to be contained within the confinement of material particularity. This expansiveness is evident in the real character of the relations between members of the same kind in which the formal likeness not only provides the basis for classification and definition but actually promotes itself in a variety of real connections: among humans, sociality, culture, politics, etc.; among animals and plants, reproduction, pairing, herd-formation, etc.; and in the inorganic realm, concentration, compounding, crystallization, and all manner of chemical interaction. The same factor of formal likeness is also the basis for real formal difference and opposition.

Both form and matter are principles of determinateness. But the determinacy brought about by form differs from that brought about by matter, as an expansive and relational principle differs from a restrictive and individuating one. Whereas material determinacy individuates, determinacy of form is not at odds with a certain bountifulness due to its immaterial character. The Schoolmen acknowledged a degree of determinism in nature, speaking of natural things as for the most part "determined to one outcome" (*determinatum ad unum*). They understood this in contrast to the liberty of choice by which rational beings have dominion over and responsibility for their acts. The new freedom, once it is freed from the critique of dogmatism and its self-referential dynamism, also suggests a more capacious universe than the early modern category of natural determinism. So, too, the determinacy of metaphysical form functions more spontaneously and vibrantly than a deterministic mechanism in the modern manner. We tend to associate form with the rigidity of quantity, reducing it to design. But the modern primacy of freedom suggests to metaphysics an expansiveness that is never without form but that moves to new formations driven by the principle of actuality (*esse actu, actus essendi*). Such hyper-determinacy is able to account for innovation, enhancing the value of novelty. It thus incorporates the new turn to history and the new awareness of the developmental character of things.[30]

An increasing sense of contingency has been characteristic of modern experience. Along with developments in probability theory in mathematics and undecidability in physics, the turn to history (occuring explicitly since the late eighteenth century) has "unsettled" the ahistorical quantitative determinism of the early modern period. But it has also suggested the generous character of being itself. This ought to permit a better understanding of the more magnanimous ancient sense of universality which held "for the most part."

Such capaciousness is not only due to the knower's inability to understand all of the complexity of a given situation; rather, it is taken to be inherent in the situation itself, not out of laxity, but instead out of the rich independence and integrity of the things in themselves. It is not,

30 One might even see in Kant's "rational faith" the admission of the inadequacy of a purely deterministic consciousness of the totality (*Totalität*); hence his definition of philosophy as an architectonic totality of knowledge (*Wissenschaft als Totalität*), of which cognition (*Erkenntnis*) is only one part.

then, a deficiency of order or a falling away from the normative guidance of form – for form is the nature of the thing as its donative principle (*forma dat esse*). Rather, form contains within itself an active potency for further determinacies that provide a certain variability within the norms pertinent to that nature. This inventiveness, always finding new refinements, is to be accredited to a positive feature rooted in the *singularity* of things. In the order of real existence, singular things perfect their composite nature, bringing both form and matter to actuality. For, unlike particularity, which only instances a thing according to its nature, singularity incorporates within itself the nature that is normative for the thing and also the matter that conditions it. The singular does not stand outside of or aside from formal order, but incorporates within itself the commonality of its form and the particularity of its matter.

Indeed, the singular possesses the transcendental properties shared by all things, by which it participates with them in the community of beings. It is important to remark that it is *participation* and not merely static possession. The participation in these transcendental properties is the basis for all manner of interaction among things, an interaction that reaches across specific boundaries and effects real results in the community of beings.

A recognition of the singularity of things is indicated, too, by recent modifications in the concept of system, away from an absolute system whose members are defined precisely and exhaustively in terms of their function within the system. As I have argued, the modern movement towards the absolute autonomy of the human subject has been complicit with the denial of integrity to other things, reducing them to objects and even to phenomena, which are then fit members of a system that encroaches upon their integrity. As things re-emerge in their singularity from such a system, a new sense of order, sensitive to the historical condition and contingency of all things, is required. This calls also for a new more concrete epistemology.[31]

The expansiveness of form is especially marked when perception comes into play. In the metaphysical understanding, all knowing is possible only through some liberation from the contraction of matter. One

31 The various distributions of meaning – from the traditional relation of universal and particular associated with metaphysics to its modern variants, such as that of generality and instance, law and case, or class and member – while serving a legitimate, partial, and secondary purpose, do not do full justice to the concrete singularity of things. I have developed this argument in more detail in "Created Receptivity and the Philosophy of the Concrete," in *The Thomist* 61 (3 July 1997): 339–71, esp. 352–6.

sees it in the perception among higher animals, where the expansiveness becomes explicit. For the animal does not live submerged and isolated in its *locus,* but senses its situation, and is aware of it in some measure that rises above restriction to and total absorption into its material conditions. The universe is not a heap of separate and isolated things. As we have said, plants reach out to nutrients, and rocks enter into chemical reaction. This liberation increases decisively in human beings, who not only perceive their situation but understand it as well, not excluding their own inevitable demise. For with human life the immaterial becomes spiritual, with its own laws of technology, culture, society, politics, art, and religion.[32]

In general, then, we see in the expansiveness of form the expression of a larger freedom built into the very constitution of things. It is, however, the modern experience and its evaluation of freedom that alerts us to an insight into a deeper and more comprehensive contextual freedom. I suggest, further, that all things are situated within a deeper spiritual medium. That medium is constituted by the spirit of creative generosity which takes the world not simply as given (*datum*) but as gift (*donum*).

It is not surprising that there are traces of the spiritual origin of the universe as gift. In the metaphysics of being, each thing participates in the freedom of its Creator with a relative freedom, relative to the spontaneity of the nature it has received. With the human being we reach the first level at which a consciously spiritual principle is at work and at which one can speak of a transcendent freedom that entails a freedom of choice. For in the order of spirit, there are no contractions of matter; all is formal and actual freedom. Nor is it simply a freedom of choice, but the very mode of spiritual being, its transcendence of the conditions of matter. Form still plays its normative role. This deeper freedom includes the moment of election, but it is more generous than a freedom exhausted by its poise between two alternatives. The very rhythm of being itself pulses with this ontological freedom. This acknowledges a deeper sense of the contingency and fluidity of things. Here freedom meets *creatio ex nihilo,* in the sense that, at the source of all intelligibility, value, and form, there pours forth the celebration of freedom.

If the universe is the gift of the Creator, then it must reflect in its depths the freedom that is native to its origins. Here the new and deeper sense of freedom is convergent with the freedom of things, not as objects given, but as gifted creatures. And so, if the created universe

32 I have made the argument for the distinctive mode of personal, spiritual existence in "The First Principle of Personal Becoming," *Review of Metaphysics* 47 (June 1994): 757–74.

has a spiritual origin, it is not surprising that the immateriality of form holds within itself a generosity that presages freedom. For the elevation of freedom beyond choice points to the original freedom that underlies a world created freely by an act of divine generosity. It is the creation as gift.[33] All things are situated within this deeper spiritual medium, a medium pervaded by freedom, by the spirit of creative generosity. The modern emphasis upon freedom helps metaphysics to see more clearly into its own resources. It permits us, too, to gather up the career of freedom into the dimensions traced out towards the end of the previous chapter, and to trace them out, not simply as the history of consciousness, but also as part of the very story of being itself. For with greater insight into the character of freedom we have the opportunity to participate more fully in its generosity. We are now in a position to appreciate that generosity, if we reclaim the dimensions of freedom that have so far shown themselves in the unitary yet threefold fullness of the teleological, normative, and conative facets of the ontology of freedom. It is this unitary fullness that offers itself as what I have called "the new freedom," once we have placed the modern insistence upon *conatus* within the fuller context of freedom that is available through a recovery of its other facets.

33 I have taken up this theme more fully in *The Gift: Creation* (Milwaukee, Wis.: Marquette University Press 1982).

Epilogue and Envoi

Nature yet remembers
What was so fugitive
Wordsworth

All that which lies outside our sort of way,
Those wordless creatures who are there as well
W.H. Auden

IN THE FOREGOING I have traced the rise and fall of a particular understanding of physical things as it moved from *pragmata* and *chrêmata* to *onta* and beyond to the recognition of *res*; and I have then traced further the gradual bleeding and bleaching out of that understanding into objects and phenomena, the pale ghosts of things, Russell's mental shadows. In the process of modern marginalization, things have lost their interiority. That is not to say that they have lost their insides, for an *inside* is not an *interior.* In recalling the older notion of immateriality, whereby within physical things there is a facet other than matter and its determinations, understood as a restrictive principle of location and continuity, I sought to retrieve the sense of interiority appropriate to things, even to calling them *subjects,* not subjects of consciousness (*subjecta mentis*), of course, but subjects of being (*supposita entis*).

When I first introduced the notion of interiority as immateriality, I developed the idea in terms of *form* as a principle, distinguishing the metaphysical sense of *forma* from the surface meaning of design, structure, or shape. The dynamic of fundamental enquiry deepens Aristotle's question *ti?* (what is it? *ti esti?*) into Thomas's question *utrum?* (whether it is? *an sit?*).[1] And this more penetrative questioning brings to light the absolutely

1 See especially *Summa theologiae* I, 44–7, which asks, among several questions: "Whether to create is to make something from nothing?" (I, 45, 1); "Whether creation is anything in the creature?" (I, 45, 3); "Whether to be created belongs to composite and subsisting things?" (I, 45, 4); "Whether it belongs to God alone to create?" (I, 45, 5); "Whether creation enters into the works of nature and art?" (I, 45, 8); "Whether the universe of creatures always existed?" (I, 46, 1); "Whether there is only one world?" (I, 47, 3).

radical, trans-formal principle of existential actuality within things (their *actus essendi,* the *esse rerum*). Once the question is raised, as with the proverbial geni out of the bottle, so, too, the existence of things can no longer be taken for granted, and a new sense of the contingency and fragility of things confronts the mind at a level deeper than the *lacrimae rerum.*

This probing attitude towards things arose, not from a Cartesian doubt about their reality, but out of the wonder at their existing at all. It is not, then, as with Descartes, *we* who suspend the actuality of things in doubt, but rather *the things themselves* that surprise us by awakening wonder in us (*theôria*); it is a deepened sense of that wonder (*thaumatzein*) which Aristotle saw to be the mother of philosophical enquiry. The even deeper insight that takes seriously the issue of actual existence discloses a factor within things that is not reducible to the quantitative indices of location in place, nor to the so-called primary qualities, that is, the mathematical properties and measurable correlations.[2]

It is obvious that physical things have an *inside*; one has only to crack a nut to see that. As modern scientific enquiry draws us further into the inside of things, we learn about their constitution in terms of chemical elements, molecular structures, atomic configurations, and, even beyond that, sub-atomic particularities. All of this constitutes the inside of physical compounds, but it does not yet touch the *interiority* within composite physical things. For as scientific analysis breaks down the chemical, molecular, atomic, and subatomic insides of physical compounds, the results of the analysis turn into objects; that is, objective analysis literally turns the insides of the particles inside-out. To be sure, this has been the fruitful trajectory of objective analysis: methodically to render smaller and smaller micro-objects and to increase our knowledge of the workings of material forces.[3] The fateful exemplar of such analysis is the epochal "splitting" of the atom. This accomplishment, however ambiguous its consequences, remains a stunning achievement along the four-hundred-year-old path that has been fuelled by the search for ultimacy in the form of elemental particles.

2 Writing on the idea of *existence* for the *Encyclopédie,* the French *philosophe,* physiocrat, and ecomomist Anne-Robert-Jacques Turgot (1727–81) reduced the meaning of the term "existence" to an exclusively spatio-temporal and phenomenal context with reference to the human self. It is significant that he did this deliberately in order to do away with the ultimate questions raised by metaphysics (precisely such a question as *an sit?*). In its place he wished to confine knowledge to the positive sciences which would then recognize only phenomena, spatio-temporal relations and the human subject.

3 Indeed, most recently, the neutrino, hitherto thought to be without mass, is now suspected of having some. Will it, too, turn out eventually to possess an "inside"?

Indeed, it was only during the twentieth century that theoretical physics gave central prominence to supplementary concepts, such as waves.[4]

It would be a mistake, however, to contrast simply the inside with the interior of physical things as though the inside is made of observable elements while the interior is alleged to possess inobservable principles; or as though the particles of modern science are directly observable whereas the metaphysical principles of things are dubious inferences. This was Beeckman's objection to Aristotelian principles.[5] Actually, however, both factors are based on observation, while neither is *immediately* observable. What is observed in micro-science is already constituted in part by certain methodological decisions regarding the selectivity of relevant evidence and the idealized manner of its formulation. Hegel has taught us that there is no such thing as immediacy of representation. The very supposition of immediacy is a curious modern fancy that would have puzzled the ancients.[6]

The principles of traditional metaphysics derive from an intellectual analysis within the horizon of being, whereas the conclusions of modern science mostly derive from a mathematical idealization of what is observed through the grid of experiment. Nor can it be said that traditional metaphysics has no method.[7] Nevertheless, there can be no doubt that each approach to nature bears a different relation to what is observed and that this difference enters into the analysis itself and into the formulation of its results. This is not strange, since observation in the service of enquiry – as distinct from casual observation – always has a point, an emphasis, a principle of discrimination and selection. One might even speak of a legitimate "bias." The empirio-mathematical approach of modern science seeks out

4 See, for example, David Bohm, *Wholeness and the Implicate Order* (London: Ark Paperbacks 1984); also, D. Schindler, ed., *Beyond Mechanism: The Universe in Recent Physics and Catholic Thought* (Lanham: University of Pennsylvania Press 1986).

5 As already mentioned, for Beeckman "macroscopic mechanical phenomena [were to] be explained in terms of microscopic mechanical processes which are essentially similar to them ... [Hence] speed and direction of motion were taken to be the basic explanatory features [of] a genuinely quantitative account." S. Gaukroger, *Descartes* (Oxford, U.K.: Clarendon 1995), 70, 72.

6 I see in the false expectation of immediacy the nominalistic drive to draw all things into simple, that is, unmediated, identity. Hegel correctly diagnosed the demand without, however, entirely freeing his own thought from nominalistic tendencies.

7 See, for example, St Thomas Aquinas, *In librum Boethii De trinitate quaestiones quinta et sexta*, edited by P. Wyser (Louvain: Nauwelaerts 1948). For the English translation by A. Maurer, CSB, see *The Division and Methods of the Sciences* 3rd ed. (Toronto: Pontifical Institute of Mediaeval Studies 1963).

the values of precision in quantitatively determinable relations, whereas the intellectual-ontological approach of traditional metaphysics seeks out the constitution of things in terms of their being and its principles.[8] Here again, we encounter a difference in the modes of discourse and the fruits of the two different analyses. In the one case, the result is a complex formulation of correlative quantities given unified expression in the laws of physics and its cognate sciences; in the other, the result is an account of composite entities in terms of the constitutive principles of form, matter, accidents, substance, essence, and existence.

We have every right to ask whether these latter notions have any basis in observation, whether they have any claim to our serious attention. We have been encouraged in the popular culture to prefer microanalysis to what might be called macroanalysis, although the latter might be more aptly called interpretation based upon direct observation. This preference is not surprising given the brilliant growth of scientific knowledge and microparticle analysis over the past four centuries and the manner in which it has transformed our lives in precisely two of the three branches named by Descartes: engineering and medicine.[9]

Any attempt simply to disparage modern development would be absurd. Nonetheless, we ought to be more aware than we often are of the logic involved in that development and the methodological decisions that support it. It is said that science demonstrates the real, but through our ordinary experience we demonstrate the existence of things every day and draw important meaning from them; indeed, these things even form the initial basis of microanalysis. Yet we are encouraged to banish such properties as colour from learned discourse on the grounds that they are "merely subjective." Colour is a property of macrocomplex things, not directly of microsimple particles. It requires an eye to be seen, but then there *are* eyes and we are talking of things as they *are* and not only as they appear to be.

8 One need not agree with Martin Heidegger's *Destruktion* of metaphysics, nor with his construal of its so-called "onto-theo-logical" understanding of entities (*das Seiende*), to recognize the merit of the issue he has raised in regard to traditional metaphysics. By rendering metaphysics problematic through his criticism, he has highlighted the transition from the quasi-mythical conceptions of the early philosophers to the ontological horizon (*on ê on*, being qua being) exploited by Plato and Aristotle. In so doing, he has brought the focus and scope of traditional metaphysics forward for explicit consideration. In a word, he has made the question of the metaphysics of being *thematic*.

9 It has not done so well in the third branch, that of ethics. Descartes promised an ethics based upon the method, but he never redeemed that promise; nor is it clear that he could.

Moreover, insofar as microanalysis is objective, it is clearly subject-dependent. And so both macro and microanalysis involve the human subject, and both endorse a method, the one less pre-determined than the other. In other words, the enquiring subject is as much involved in microanalysis as it is in macroanalysis. It is a methodological decision that relegates certain macroproperties (the so-called secondary qualities) to the "merely subjective," letting our imaginations be carried away in favour of the "objectivity" of microanalysis. But, if "objectivity" results from a methodological decision that favours certain epistemic values, such as precision and quantitative variables, we need to be aware of the logic inherent in that decision and its "thinning out" of things in disregard of the "thick" things before our very eyes. In justice, then, let each method play itself out in accordance with its own competence and values, the one of quantitative precision, the other of ontological realities.

Both approaches are needed, for while this is a universe in which there are micro-particles, it is also a universe in which there are things every bit as real as the particles and far richer in meaning, value, and presence – present as they are in so many varied ways and with interior depth. For, whereas metaphysics makes no claim to predictive power or precision, it does demand confirmation in and through experience. That is why the results of metaphysical analysis can lay claim to our serious attention, provided that we attend to rather basic observable facts and confine our attention to them.

First fact: things often change without completely losing their identity; this identity-factor is the subtratum (*substantia, suppositum*) that undergoes and remains throughout their coming-to-be in some particular way or other, as when trees change from green to brown. Second fact: things originate from anterior conditions, some of which are causes; these are pro-genitors (the *causa efficiens*), as trees grow from seeds, sun, water, and other nutrients. Third fact: things exhibit patterns of regularity; these are due to their natures (the *causa formalis*), as certain kinds of trees for the most part flower in certain seasons. Fourth fact: things in varying degree have the consistency and persistence to remain in existence; this is their primary orientation (the *causa finalis*), as weeds brook our energetic attempts to dig them out of the lawn. These kinds of facts are accumulated over a more or less extended experience of things.

With these, I have just enumerated the staple concepts of traditional metaphysics: *substance, cause, nature,* and *finality*. The observations that ground these concepts are neither precise nor directly productive of a tangible result. They are humble in their simplicity, familiarity, and obviousness. The observations and the concepts drawn from them lack the precision of scientific investigations, but then they do not strive for such precision; their excellence lies elsewhere. Nor are they so directly productive as modern technology: philosophical knowledge bakes no bread. But philosophy can affect the baker and the way he treats his materials. And so it is not self-evident that such analysis should be simply branded as otiose, as Hobbes and the positivists are wont to do.

Instead of dismissing such analysis outright without further ado, as though it belongs to the infancy of the race or even to its dark ages, we might ask whether it – or something like it – may not, after all, play a distinctive role and serve an important purpose.[10] For, if metaphysical notions are not productive, they *are* practical in that they can quietly shape our basic attitude towards the world in which we live, setting up a recursive relation with the world which in turn affects us. In so doing, *theôria* and *praxis* converge to shape our mutual relation with others, both with things and with persons.

Though, in the modern way of thinking, things have lost their interiority, interiority itself seems to be an aspect that cannot be entirely done away with without reducing all meaning to nonsense in the literal etymology of that word.[11] In short, interiority is an indispensable and privileged attribute. That is why it did not disappear entirely in the modern

10 Eugen Fink (*Sein, Wahrheit, Welt: Vor-Fragen zum Problem des Phänomen-Begriffes* [The Hague: Martinus Nijhoff/Phaenomenologica 1958]) has remarked that a culture can exist without modern science but not without some form of ultimate questioning. In many cultures, religion plays that role. In our own culture, such questioning exists often either in cooperation or in tension with religion. Traditional metaphysics is the methodical effort, born of the Greeks, to enquire into such questions.

11 This is the attack directed against metaphysics by the positivists in the earlier part of this past century, such as Alfred J. Ayer in his early work, *Language, Truth and Logic* (repr. New York: Dover 1952). More recently, some linguists have sought to reduce language to a system of signs without any or minimal reference to their conceptual content. Such a view seems espoused by Jacques Derrida, who writes of a theory of language whose basis lies below the threshold of meaning. Language then will have retreated, first from its relation to truth and then from its relation to meaning. It will have ceased to be a medium of communication and have become a means for social empowerment. See the essay "The Ends of Man" in K. Baynes *et al.*, ed., *After Philosophy: End or Transformation?* (Cambridge Mass.: MIT 1987): "It is a question of determining the possibility of *meaning* on the basis of a 'formal' organization that in itself has no meaning" (150). No doubt, Derrida has in mind his own sense of language, which includes the withdrawal from both signifier and signified, but it seems to me that the thrust towards language as social tactic is at work in the general culture as well; and it also seems to me that this is a reversion to rhetoric in place of *theôria*.

period; it merely sought refuge in one or another form of consciousness.[12] What remained of diminished interiority during modern times was reserved to the human consciousness exclusively: the thinker in Descartes, the sensory recipient in Hume, the critical reason in Kant, the Absolute Spirit in Schelling and Hegel, transcendental subjectivity in Husserl. This exclusive identification of interiority with human consciousness is at the starting point of the logical path by which both subjective status and interiority are withdrawn from things and reserved to the human subject.[13]

As already alluded to in reference to Kant, the modern project seeks mastery of nature as much for confirmation of its new sense of self as it does in order to dominate things; concretely, it seeks the new sense of self-empowerment in and through its mastery of things. For it seeks control in order to realize possibilities of freedom that have not hitherto existed for humankind. There can be no doubt that the logic of modernity has played a significant role in altering the human condition in many ways for the better, even beyond what its modern initiators might have imagined. But, as with all human endeavours, ambivalence dogs its advance. Indeed, it might be said that it has succeeded almost too well. And with the triumph of modernity, freedom has embedded itself within the very texture of modern society: as partially, if ambiguously, realized in the so-called advanced societies, and as an ideal that is pursued in many others.

By freedom, however, as already mentioned, I do not mean only individual deliberation about choices, or even collective freedom about alternatives. For modern freedom is deeply and broadly entrenched in post-industrial technologies in a variety of less obvious ways. Thus, freedom is present in these ways, not simply through the choices that may

12 Thus engendering a reaction in the form of behaviourism and other denials of consciousness as a distinctive mode of psychic reality, such as the reduction of thought processes to brain synapses. One recalls Ryle's refutation of the "ghost in the machine," aimed at Cartesian dualism. For my own defence of the distinctive character of consciousness which also rejects Cartesian dualism, see "The First Principle of Personal Becoming" in *The Review of Metaphysics* 47 (June 1994): 757–74.

13 It is just this modern introspection that has come under attack from postmodern thinkers, such as Derrida, who tend to replace it with language interpreted as an interlocking field of differential signs. Modern thought, having driven interiority back into the human psyche, is now subjected by postmodern criticism to the attempt to annihilate interiority entirely. This has as its cognate theme the death of man and all forms of humanism. In more literary fashion, Alain Robbe-Grillet, in the novel *Jealousy* (London: Calder 1959, repr. 1987) draws out a sustained description of the surfaces of the surrounding milieu, deliberately eschewing any reference to depth.

have entered into their establishment, but in their exercise and execution, so that they have become constituent in the very being of these modern ways of life. Individuals living in a modern society enter into them, not by choice, but by accepting a modern way of life: living out the mobility of modern transportation, the ease of telecommunication, freedom from the threat of many diseases, increased longevity of life, the devolution of some centres of power, and the abundance of consumer goods.

And yet the very moment of its seeming triumph is a moment of great danger for the continuance of the modern ideal and the cultivation of the freedom that it aims to advance. For the path of modern freedom is an ambiguous one. Indeed, it may seem callous to herald the advent of a new freedom in the past century, which saw more death and devastation than any other, more violations of human dignity, more forced uprooting of peoples, the tyranny of totalitarian regimes armed with the latest technological weapons of mass dehumanization, and increased terrorist activity often done in the name of a particular version of freedom.

Nevertheless, despite all of this, there are voices – still small but increasing in volume – that call for reflection and restraint in our approach to things. At the sober core of this reflection there is no nostalgic complaint about the benefits of the massive technological power that has been accumulated alongside an ideal of personal and social liberty that is sometimes in conflict with it. There is, however, a growing realization of the enormity of that technical power.

One instance may suffice to sharpen the appreciation of its enormity. When settlers first came to the region near the shores of Lake Ontario, they were confronted by the wilderness, an immense tangle of all but impenetrable forest. The wilderness was a reality to be feared, since the ever-encroaching mass of trees posed great danger to human beings, to wandering children, to lost adults starved or frozen or mauled by animals. The wilderness was a forbidding and resistant barrier to colonization and to fertile fields. Nowadays, on the contrary, the national government sets up large areas, some of them the size of small countries, in the north and west of Canada as "wilderness parks," with limited access to the general public. By so doing it attempts to protect the pristine wilderness from the devastating effects of casual and merely curious human intrusion. Protector and protected have been reversed. We have here a radical inversion of the natural and the human, of the power of nature and the power of man. To the previous inversion of thought over things (signalled by Descartes) and the inversion of freedom over cognition (signalled by Kant), we now add a third inversion: that of technological power over nature, at whose root is an ambiguous relation to a fully human freedom. Despite the ability of nature to deal devastating blows on occasion, an almost unlimited accretion of technical power threatens to carry us into increasingly troubled straits in our relation with things.

There is, of course, a body of literature on environmental and ecological issues – the best being based upon careful scientific research – that takes up such problems as climate change, resource depletion, biodiversity, and the like. These bear upon the nature and status of things, and it is to this latter concern that philosophy may add its word. Among recent philosophers there are several who sound a warning about the indiscriminate use of technological power. Notable among these in the past century is the French philosopher Gabriel Marcel (1889–1974).[14] In *The Decline of Wisdom* he insists that he is not raising a tiresome and nostalgic appeal for "the good old days" when he notices the drastic destruction of the contours of the earth which is observed in some places in Latin America and which is replicated elsewhere in urban sprawl. He argues that such power, drawn from and modelled largely upon the modality of physical power, without respect for bio-forms and animal life,[15] has too often overridden personal values to the detriment of more ample human relations. Among the more extreme examples Marcel mentions are the "techniques of degradation" practised, not only in the Europe of sixty or seventy years ago by totalitarian regimes, but in many other places today. He also instances more subtle forms closer to home that subordinate personal values and vulnerable human associations, such as family and neigbourhood, to the demands of impersonal functional utility and short-term aims.

At a deeper level, Marcel calls for a meta-technical or trans-technical mode of thought which seeks to situate action within a more expansive context than immediate technical control and the manipulation of objects. He calls that context "the mystery of being" – mysterious, in part, because it resists all our attempts to bottle it up within abstract systems of

14 See, for example, Gabriel Marcel's *Man against Mass Society*, (trans. G.S. Fraser; Chicago: Henry Regnery/Gateway 1962), whose original French title dramatically points up the issue: *Les hommes contre l'humain*. See also his *Decline of Wisdom* (London: Harvill Press 1954), where he makes clear that he is not sounding a tiresome complaint against technology as such but only calling for a reflection upon its limits and appropriate use.

15 The problems of pollution brought on by chemical-waste lagoons and mass meat-farm factories are becoming more obvious, as poisoned soil and water endanger human habitation through the assault upon organic and inorganic modes of existence. Nor is it mere sentimentality to feel a profound sadness at the sight of animals treated as no more than appendages to the alimentary canal.

technical thought, and also because it constantly draws our thought out of itself into existential encounters with a horizon in which we find ourselves but which overreaches us on all sides. Marcel raises a call for a meta-technical wisdom against the backdrop of modern idealism.[16] His argument implies a deep sensibility and respect for the inherent dignity of things, seen through the optics of respect for the person. And so, even if his perspective does not explicitly address the recovery of the full reality of things considered in themselves as embodiments of being, the strength of his own strategy is that it disengages human reality from its identification with a Cartesian methodic or Kantian transcendental a priori subjectivity. For, as we have seen, such an understanding of human reality prevails over the dignity of things, turning them into objects standing, not only over against or simply subordinate to, but wholly at the disposal of the human *ego.*

Foremost in Marcel's critique of the current domination of technical modes of thought is the *malaise* of the ordinary person who is immersed in the busyness of his work-a-day world, with little time or grounds for deeper reflection. Surely, it is not an accident that our "free" time is referred to as a "vacation," that is, as "empty, vacant time." A brief excerpt from Marcel's essay "On the Ontological Mystery" may convey something of the tone of his concern with the frantic pace of much of modern life: "The characteristic feature of our age seems to me to be what might be called the misplacement of the idea of function [so many hours for each function] ... The individual tends to appear both to himself and to others as an agglomeration of functions ... [vital, social, economic, political] ... There is the dull, intolerable unease of the [individual] who is reduced to living as though he were in fact submerged by his functions. This uneasiness is enough show that there is in all this some appalling mistake ...[17]

Somewhat in the same vein are the writings of Ortega y Gasset, who maintains that the uniformity and standardization so prevalent in modern life has replaced authentic diversity with a plethora of superficial

16 Marcel frames his argument against the backdrop of his rejection of idealism in its Cartesian and Kantian forms, whereas my present argument moves within a more traditional metaphysical realism. For a correlation between Marcel's "existential" reflection and metaphysical realism, see my article "The Solidarity of Personalism and the Metaphysics of Existential Act," *Fides Quaerens Intellectum,* 1, 1 (summer 2001): 183–99.

17 *The Philosophy of Existentialism,* trans. by Manya Harari, 6th ed. (New York: Citadel Press/Philosophical Library 1966), 10–12. A similar reflection in a more traditional metaphysical mode is that of Josef Pieper, *Leisure the Basis of Culture* (trans. Alexander Dru; New York: Pantheon Books 1952).

variety. (What comes to mind is a recent television add that promises 350 "different" channels and over a thousand movies!). The *personalist* movement is critical of pan-technicism and technocracy, the rule of techniques, and – lacking the recovery and renewal of a more deeply grounded traditional metaphysics – seeks to retrieve the dignity of the environs through attention to the dignity of the person without explicitly addressing the present topic of the proper status of things. Nevertheless, the atmosphere in which its critical thought moves is thoughtfully sensitive to the *malaise* of the modern person studied by Marcel. And so it is not unfriendly to the needed respect for the integrity of things which can play a corrective role in contributing to a richer human life.

What is required for such a meta-technical wisdom, however, is not simply a change in regard to the ontolgoical status of things – a new context respecting their integrity and dignity – but a change in the way in which we view things. And that calls for a recovery of the ancient attitude of *theoria*: a receptive – but not a merely passive – disposition towards the world in which we live.[18] Modern thought is attentive to its empirical base; for, as Kant says in the preface to the *Critique of Pure Reason*, we must not ascribe to nature whatever we might wish, but must base our reasoning on the data that comes to us from the senses. He adds, however, that we must not listen to *everything* that nature has to tell us; rather, we must constrain nature to conform to a conceptual scheme that lies within us and that is prior to any observation of data. The original theoretical attitude, on the other hand – while not easy to attain – entrains a willingness to listen to nature with as open a mind as possible. Indeed, scientific geniuses often attain such openness, even within the focus of their own discipline. But is one thing for an individual to adopt such an attitude and quite another for a culture or society to do so and to reflect that attitude in its policy decisions – especially a society that prizes precision, control, and manipulative power as among its highest values. For, if we let nature speak to us without pre-determined demands, we may be in for surprises. Yet our desperate attempt to stifle

18 Marcel's notion of *receptivity* (*reçevoir, disponibilité;* the latter rendered as "availability"; "The Ontological Mystery" in *The Philosophy of Existentialism*) is helpful here. By that term he means an attitude toward the other that is not merely passive but rather an attentive disposition towards the presence of the other. He finds that the active-passive dichotomy – which he concedes is evident at the material and physical level of being (though I should want to qualify this in keeping with the spontaneity inherent in things) – diminishes as we consider more complex modes of existence. Thus, we speak of a host "receiving" a guest; and by that we do not mean after the manner of wax passively conforming to the imprint of the seal, but rather that the host is actively attentive to the presence of his/her guest.

nature by the attempt to submit it to an excessive and nearly absolute technical control is showing us surprises as well – and most of them unwelcome ones at that, in the form of mutating viruses, unintended consequences, and the like. It must be made clear, of course, that specific aims directed towards nature, whether in the interest of practical utility or in that of a better understanding of particular problems, is not to be discouraged. What is called for is the restoration of our particular addresses to nature (that is, the various sciences) within a revised general attitude of respect towards it. This calls for, not just an ineffectual and well-meaning admiration, but a respect by which we permit nature to set certain limits to our exploitation of it.

The appropriate social and cultural solution seems to be neither the attempt at absolute subordination of nature to human control nor the total abandonment of all attempts to shape nature in conformity with our own legitimate needs and desires. What is needed, rather, is a more discriminating reserve in the application of technical expertise to borderline experiments with natural things and human persons. Too often we accept the Promethean maxim: "If it can be done, it must be done." A better maxim might well be: "Enhance nature along nature's rhythms in accord with our legitimate needs." A general rule might well be to intervene in natural processes both to correct defects and also to facilitate the workings of nature – but along the lines and dynamisms of natural processes and not in contravention of them. To the maxim we hear too often – "Just do it!!" – we might suggest a counter-maxim: "It is better to facilitate the productive workings of nature by listening to its voice" – not by coercing it but by correcting it where defective and enhancing it along the borders of its own impetus. This would still leave much room for human creativity and innovation. The model would be that of a "physician of nature," curing and caring for it rather than simply dominating it.

Such a companionate attitude and practice would call for an educational tradition that encourages innovation but also respects the given tendencies of nature. It would encourage a more circumspect consideration of long-range consequences over against immediate but ultimately only apparent and ambiguous gains. This would call for a new motivation, more patient, yet active in the wondering discovery of nature and its processes, and less frantically domineering. It is not incidental that, in social policy, while we have developed a spatial vocabulary to describe political motivation and direction (we speak of left, right, and centre tendencies), we have given relatively little thought to the temporal pace of social and cultural change. Yet, if the pace is too swift, we not only undermine the credibility of existing institutions, we may also bring down on our heads natural consequences of a most unwelcome sort, such as unnecessary pollution, uncontrollable disease, a growing gap between rich and poor, perhaps even unwanted climate change.

The present condition calls for a rethinking of the modern sanction of "progress." As already indicated, nature itself is teaching us by way of unfortunate consequences of a too hasty and indiscriminate use of technical power. And indeed, in the so-called "advanced societies," the present generation is more aware than previous ones that a technical gain may have unintended side-effects. Once again, it cannot be said too often, this is not a complaint against modern technology but rather a plea for a more considered use of it. In any general cultural change of attitude, valuation, and motivation, many parties in society need to join in the reappraisal – not least the artists, musicians, and poets, whose imaginative creations have the power to move us. Indeed, the poetic headings with which each chapter in the present work begins are placed there, not as mere elegant decorations, but as testimony to a residual wisdom that is still in the keeping of poets, novelists, and other creative artists. We need everyone, and not least those talented in the modern art forms, such as cinema, television, and the Internet, to dramatize the human possibilities awaiting a more open and respectful attitude towards things – new advocates for a more companionate love of things.

The more sober of what is as yet a small number of cautionary voices are calling for a new appreciation of things. The call is often, and understandably, motivated by fear: that the loss of species will denude the earth of colourful interest and variety; that the loss of forests will lead to climatic and atmospheric changes endangering health; that overproduction will lead to impoverishment of arable lands and even to desertification; that pollution will kill the rivers and poison the land and air. These voices call for each new advance in technology to be scrutinized for its unwanted side-effects. The white lab coat so prominent in past commercials is no longer uncritically accepted as an authority symbol. An awareness is growing that, with each new technical solution, new problems may be expected to emerge: antibiotic resistant viruses, uncontrolled urbanization, exhaustion of soils – the list is familiar to us all. And yet our society finds all but irresistible the maxim that, if something can be done, it must be done. If we can clone, we must clone. It is the maxim that maximizes technique and technical power often in undiscriminating ways.

Initially it may be thought that a certain technique cannot be done; when it can be done, too often the pressure "to just do it" is resisted by moral negatives: it ought not to be done. But these admonitions need a deeper support, especially when they are presented as rules to be observed. A second attempt at prohibition then spells out the purported negative consequences, raising the spectre of fear. We might ask, however, whether there are more positive grounds for a critical reassessment of the maxim.

Certainly, fear is a salutary motive for human conduct. In respect to such a massive socio-cultural change of attitude as is characteristic of modern life, however, it is at least questionable whether fear alone is enough to move us to contain this unprecedented power within tolerable human limits. Are there other grounds, in concert with but more positive than fear, for bringing the application of such power to a more discriminate use?

What is needed is a new asceticism of power. And that asceticism needs to be motivated by more than the fear of consequences: such as the loss of aesthetic variety of natural surroundings, or the loss of habitat for certain human groups, or the loss of specific resources. For such consequences may appear rather more distant than imminent, or may seem to affect only a few and not those remote from the immediate concern, appearing to leave unaffected more powerful vested interests.

What is more, in falling back on fear, the list simply re-enacts the recursive withdrawal into self that has driven modern thought and society into the present straits. While moved by the fear of consequences, the new asceticism of power must be grounded in a new attitude to things which respects in them their interiority and their depth – in a word, their appropriate integrity. May we even speak of a love of things, as the poet Rupert Brooke did? Not a love tinged with sentimentality, but a tougher, more realistic love, a love that sponsors our mutual well-being. Things themselves are calling us to such realism. And so ought we not to search for a new sense of solidarity with things that, after all, are our unavoidable companions on this planet? A *companionate love,* then.

Such an attitude of respect for things would bring us out of ourselves, would inspire a certain radiation beyond ourselves. To be sure, it is unlikely that such a reorientation can be sustained by a change of ideas alone. Intellectual insight must be clothed with imagery and enlivened by a new sensibility if it is to move us; so that ideas embedded in the creative powers can at best serve as tiny seeds for such a change. Here the philosopher must give way to the citizen and politician, but also to the poet, the novelist, and the artist, in the hope that eventually our laws and policies will reflect a greater appreciation for the interiority of things. A certain refusal to acknowledge a transcendent dimension is inherent in the project of modernity; it is an arbitrary confinement of the horizon of thought and action to the human dimension narrowly conceived. As a philosophy, whether stated or not, such a denial defines the narrow scope of secular humanism. Public discussions in the so-called modernized societies usually proceed with at best minimal consideration of a trans-human, that is, a transcendent dimension inherent in the issues, as though only immediate relations with the individual or collective human subject are worthy of consideration.

The mere mention of a dimension that transcends the circle of human subjectivity may make some otherwise decent and intelligent people nervous. They suspect a hidden agenda and protest against its inclusion in any public discussion. Here, we should first note that transcendence has two centrifugal foci: the one is towards nature, as when we go out to things; the other is towards the sacred, as when we acknowledge a larger and more ultimate reality. As to acknowledgement of a sacred reality that transcends human concerns, there is a well-developed secularist mythology, not without its partial truth, that resists what it takes to be an unwarranted intrusion into the public domain of what it assesses as mere private opinion in the form of religious belief. Public prayer is often treated as, at best, a residual formality and, at worst, a practice that is increasingly irrelevant and even offensive to many.

The first condition for altering such a view must be openly acknowledged by religious believers: it calls for a convincing renunciation by all religious institutions and individuals of any attempt to use coercive and intimidating power. Only the power of the spirit is appropriate in the realm of the transcendent: and that is the power of the truth arrived at freely through dialogue and example. Moreover, religious adherents need to recognize that the process of modernization has been accompanied by an expanded sense of freedom in regard to ultimate issues. As a result, the career of modernization has released the human spheres of politics and public affairs from inappropriate religious interventions. However, this should not justify the arbitrary exclusion of all consideration of transcendence from human affairs. It is odd that many who think of themselves as liberal welcome the free competition of ideas and their truth-value while at the same time simply refusing to admit religious ideas into that conversation.

As for the second focus of transcendence – the focus towards things – we have to recognize that transcendence towards nature is not likely to occur as long as the natural world is conceived as a system of objects or as a field of phenomena. The movement outward towards things can be effectively motivated only if things are seen to contain that thickness and depth that makes them worthy of consideration in and for themselves. Yet explicit acknowledgement of transcendence has been all but rejected, in favour of a movement that closes in on human subjectivity in a kind of airless circle. As a result, by rejecting both the transcendence of nature and the transcendence of the sacred, the modern aspiration for freedom is itself curtailed, even though it is nurtured in many other ways by the modern project.

In sum, the process of secularization has brought with it, sometimes intended sometimes not, the ideology of a practical secularism. Such an ideology abruptly banishes the consideration of any transcendent reality, reducing it without argument to mere private opinion which is not permitted even a hearing in public discussions. Even when it does not degenerate into the ideology of secular humanism, such practical secularism breathes with the spirit of modern objectivity and self-enclosed subjectivity. It withdraws the sense of interiority from things and denies them their status as ontological subjects, once again closing the circle of self-reference too quickly upon the individual or collective human subject. This leaves us with the political alternatives of an extreme individualism (classical liberalism) or extreme collectivism (classical statism), neither of which promote the full freedom so precious to modern experience.

With the elevation of the human subject to primacy – as *subjectum fundamentum inconcussum* – and the consequent bleaching out of what I have called the "thick" sense of things, those very things have lost their integrity, that is, their wholeness; for if interiority is denied, so too is integrity. On this one point, traditional metaphysics, religion, and the secular humanism of the Enlightenment agree: the empowerment that is appropriate to integrity derives from interiority. Of course, each defines the *locus* of interiority in its own way. Religion finds the source of interiority and integrity ultimately in the sacred, metaphysics finds integrity and interiority derivatively in the things themselves grounded in an interior depth that points beyond them towards an ultimate source, whereas the secular rationalism of the Enlightenment denies interiority and integrity to things and locates them in the human psyche. According to it, objects, devoid of their own interiority and integrity and hence of their proper empowerment, merely stand over against the human subject as plastic material whose meaning is to serve human ends.

It is as though a new form of slavery has emerged in modern times: not the bondage of human beings to other human beings, but the bondage of things to humanity. We become no longer stewards of nature but its unrivalled masters. This is a new and dangerous option for humankind, hitherto not available because technology had not accumulated such power over nature. The price we have paid for our insistence upon the autonomy of the human sphere and the independence of the individual is a high one, and one that – if the older view of things is in some way true – should not be paid; for the loss of the integrity of things is correlative with a certain loss of our own integrity, inasmuch as we, too, are things, even if of a distinctive kind.

We live in the midst of a world of physical things and the way we value them rebounds upon our self-evaluation. If things are denied their genuine interiority, there can be no basis for our sharing a common though analogously diverse interiority with them. Perhaps, however, we are coming, if not to the end of modernity as some postmodernists tell us, at least to a new phase of it. For in some quarters there are increasing signs of just such an attempt to establish a rapport with things, even though dominant modes of thought still lag behind these attempts. Such attempts are usually driven by fear of the consequences of technology. What such efforts sometimes, but by no means always, lack is that they are undisciplined and vulnerable to foolish excesses, as when animals and plants are given more credit than human beings. It is not only our own fear, however, that prompts us; nature itself is pressing its demands upon us for a better appreciation of things. It is as though we are seated at a gaming table only to find that other players – the things of nature – are dealing us some rather unpleasant cards. Where appreciation does not extend beyond the utility of things (their *bonum utile*), what Schiller called a *moral* culture, and what is better called an *ontological* culture, will not arise.[19]

The metaphysical concept of physical things may seem archaic, but it is not simply undisciplined or without a firm intellectual basis. In order to arrive at a more humane environment and a more adequate ecology, and in order to balance our new power with our new freedom, we need to retrieve some sense of the integrity and interiority of things, of the immateriality (*forma*) and the actuality (*esse actu*) within them. I do not suggest that we put new wine in old skins, or even that we put old wine in new skins, for the Middle Ages are past. We cannot, nor should we, strive to reconstruct its associations and connotations, but we can profit from looking at some of its basic insights and principles. Perhaps the

19 The modern sense of the utility of things (qua objects) differs from the ancient sense of *ta chrêmata* and *ta pragmata* insofar as the Greeks placed these within a cosmos whose supervening quality was itself in a deep sense sacred and not simply at the disposition of human power.

relative weakness of technological power in that era left room for a clearer insight into the independence of things, as it does in some traditional societies today. What is indispensable is that, fully aware of the benefits of science and technology, we recognize a deeper solidarity with the things that surround us.

Among the ideas from the past that recommend themselves to us for further reflection is the notion that we participate with things in certain universally shared properties. Setting aside the dualistic notion of mentality or spirituality inherited from Descartes, we might recognize that the non-dualistic immateriality of form gives to the physical thing a *lambent lustre* that is the glint of its intelligibility, and an expansive *generosity* that cannot be confined within any single localized individual. For the *kind* of thing that a thing is is not merely a mental category that we formulate for our convenience. Its kind is, rather, a reality that brings the thing into real relations with other things in dynamic interaction, whether it is intra-species breeding among animals that share the same species or the chemist at work with the properties of various elements. This is the *communitas rerum,* in which we, too, have our place. Through the interior depth in things, then, there is a shared bond for mutual relations between us and things: an openess for meditation, for *theôria,* and for a wonder that grows upon us as a kind of realization of the *significance* of each thing (*res*). From that should follow a new behaviour towards things.

An appreciation of the mutuality of ourselves and things restores a sense of our co-existence with them. And within that sense of co-existence we are invited to rethink Kant's deliverance of reason from the dogmatism of things. We might ask, then: What *hubris* entitles human reason to play its role as controller at the deepest level of its relation with the world of things? I mean at the level of the "deep-down freshness" in things. The double role – in which the knower is both a party to the relation with things and also the controller who sets the conditions under which the thing is to be considered – is appropriate at secondary levels, where partial results and limited objectives are sought for; but it is inappropriate at the open level of the original encounter with things; and it is to just such an encounter that metaphysics is called. The double role may be reinstated but only on the basis of an appreciation of the deeper reality in things.

All learned discourse has its own focus, but the commitment of metaphysics to fundamental enquiry is such that the horizon of being remains radically open, providing we are ready to recognize that historical development in reality and in our understanding is part of the history of being.[20] What is misplaced here, then, is not strictly the double relation by which the knower is both a party to the relation with things and also the source of a certain particular interest in that relation. Rather, it is the character of that interest, as when despotic control is conferred a priori upon human subjectivity as master of things. What is needed is not the dissolution of the human subject's interest in the relation, for that may express a legitimate concern, even that of utility. Rather, what is needed is an interest in the mutuality of our membership in the community of beings, a mutuality that first demands *theôria* as the attitude of open encounter, listening, and respect.

Even within modern science, it is those encounters with radically new insights that characterize the theoretical thrust of so-called pure science. And the really great scientists are moved by wonder. There can be no complaint against the effort of scientists to awaken to the wonder of the universe, though it is not the task of science to push the enquiry to its most fundamental levels. The foregoing strictures, however, are directed towards a constructivist philosophy that pre-empts that wonder by foreclosing the radical openness of the encounter in favour of a prior determination regarding the structure of things, such as when the decisive features of things are taken to be only their quantifiable properties or their utility for human purposes. Only with partial aims in mind does human consciousness have the right to assume the role of judge advocate in relation to things, and only if the results are accepted as partial and selective and the larger context of the integrity of things is acknowledged and still in play. What passes as acceptable in the special sciences may not meet the requirements of philosophy as fundamental enquiry into the nature of things. For what is at issue is not simply an affront to the integrity of things but also the shortchanging of what is the fully human good (*bonum honestum*).

Because the presumption to absolute mastery is unwarranted, it sets in motion the reductionist trajectory of the regressive withdrawal of intelligibility and value from things in the interest of a reason that is in

20 I have elsewhere set out the distinction of levels of discourse, using the terms "noetic" for the first-order open attitude towards the original experience of things, and "epistemic" for the second order, deliberately selective and methodical investigation of things, such as is carried out in science and technology. While metaphysics is a learned discourse, its commitment to fundamental enquiry is such that the horizon of being is radically open and expressive of first order discourse. See my "Metaphysics: Radical, Principled, Comprehensive Thinking," *Review of Metaphysics* 39 (June 1986): 675–94; and "Neither with nor without Foundations," *Review of Metaphysics* 42 (September 1988): 3–25, esp. 14–16.

search of epistemic *security* and the guarantee of human commodiousness. It is, therefore, a reason that seeks to minimize risk by forestalling exposure to the vicissitudes of the world. Such a delimitation does not only affect human reason; it constitutes a particular view of human life. It proposes a particular anthropology. We may ask whether such a restricted anthropology does justice to the immeasurable facets of human life that are not ordered to the primary purpose of utility and comfort. In the experience of the sublime, Kant thought that freedom would be recognized in its own sphere, as long as the weight of things did not oppress it. It is a tougher, more realistic and demanding freedom that takes into account its situatedness within a world whose things possess their own dignity and value, their own weight, a weight that belongs to them by virtue of their possession of being.

As we have already seen, the Schoolmen associated certain transcendental and omnipresent characteristics with being. They called these trans-categorial characteristics by several names. The feature that is the source of the *intelligibility* of things, they called *truth* (*verum*). It is the capacity in things to respond to the questions with which we approach them and even to draw those questions out of us.[21] The very possibility of the life of intelligence, including modern science itself, rests upon the capacity of things to contribute to our questions and answers in our continuing search for meaning and truth. In this search, the integrity of things rooted in their interiority also issues an invitation to acknowledge in them an actual *value* beyond utility, a power to attract us that presents itself as a good within its proper context: thus, as Kant saw, the prodigious energy displayed by nature elicits admiration from us even as it escapes any design we might place upon it. The Schoolmen called this trans-categorial property the transcendental *good* (*bonum*), not necessarily good for us (*bonum utile*), but worthy of respect in itself, as when we admire the gait of a tiger but prefer the gate to be closed.

It is this power or actuality in things that engenders wonder in us.[22] It is this that arouses in us an admiration even when nature goes against us, as in Kant's experience of the sublime. But we do not simply experience the superiority of our freedom through the independence and resistance of things; we recognize instead a kind of secret mutual bond, and we also sense the thickness of that bond. Finally, things quicken with a *luminosity*

21 See "Natural Value," *Review of Metaphysics* 38 (September 1984): 3–15.

22 Taken in the broadest sense, this is more than a moral good (*bonum morale*) and is properly an ontological good, that good which belongs to a thing insofar as it possesses being (*bonum honestum* in the broadest sense). See Thomas Aquinas, *Summa theologiae* I, q. 5, a. 6c and ad 3.

and *effulgence* that expresses a distinctive configuration. To this characteristic, which escapes the confines of species and transgresses the formal limits of the thing even as it heightens their formal quality, the Schoolmen gave the name, beauty (*pulchrum*). It is that which we admire in the graceful movement of an animal, or the swaying of trees in the wind, beyond any utility these might have for us.[23] It is the grace that invites us to celebrate the rhythm of things, the call to music, poetry, and art. It is the very "dance" of things. To turn the lines of T.S. Eliot's *Burnt Norton* to the present purpose: "At the still point" – in the quiet of contemplation (*theôria*) – "there the dance is."

These transcendental characteristics are gathered together in the humble thing even as they overflow its individuality and its specific determinacy. This is what metaphysics means by the seemingly dry formula *ens et verum et bonum et pulchrum convertuntur.* Spelt out, it means that, wherever one finds being, one also finds the knowable (*verum*), the valuable (*bonum*), and the beautiful (*pulchrum*), though the ontological good and the beautiful may not always be convenient for us. It points, too, to an intrinsic otherness (*aliquid*) in things that incorporates an interior relatedness in them by which they participate analogously in the community of beings. These facets make up the texture of being, which resists and survives the assaults of every loss of meaning, value, and beauty, even as it suffers them.

Past ages celebrated these transcendental properties, not from a narrowly defined sense of human relevance and utility, or from a naive disregard of privation and things gone wrong, for they certainly knew the ugliness and deformity that often defaces things. They knew, too, the *lacrimae rerum,* and the poet's reminiscence: "to look on nature … hearing often times the still, sad music of humanity." But they saw through evil to a grander vision of the majesty of the universe. For the quality of *verum* secures the intelligibility of the world of things, *bonum* its value and *pulchrum* its luminosity.

Even today, these properties of the reality of things invite us to look beyond their familiar presence to the mystery of things themselves: and in *seeing them anew* we are invited to recover the wondrous splendour that gives rise to *theôria.* It is in the recognition of our solidarity with things (*aliquid*) that we find a fuller freedom. Through the inclination that is inherent in us we are drawn towards the otherness of things (the teleology of freedom); through our nature and theirs we are guided by norms embedded in both them and us (the normativity of freedom);

23 This is a form of the *bonum delectabile,* the good that delights.

and through the originative power resident in us we have the opportunity to live with them in a creative way (the conativity of freedom). Such an integrated freedom does not divide us from things or set us over against nature; instead it situates us with other things in the midst of an ontological community.

In tracing the story of the thing, we have come face to face with the native character of our freedom. In restoring to things their dignity and depth, and their claim upon us, we come to understand ourselves and our freedom better. A philosophical reflection such as this, insofar as it has substantial truth in it, is the work of many, not of one; it is the elaboration of a culture. The philosopher simply comes along and draws the threads together into the fabric of our freedom in the midst of things. In telling that story we recover in an intellectual mode the wonder that is the poetry of the world.

Index

N.B. p 67 – The separation of thought from the world